FILM STARS

Stars are an integral part of the global film industry. This is as true today, in the age of celebrity culture, as in the studio era. Each book in this major new BFI series focuses on an international film star, tracing the development of their star persona, their career trajectory and their acting and performance style. Some also examine the cultural significance of a star's work, as well as their lasting influence and legacy. The series ranges across a wide historical and geographical spectrum, from silent to contemporary cinema and from Hollywood to Asian cinemas, and addresses both child and adult stardom.

SERIES EDITORS
Martin Shingler and Susan Smith

PUBLISHED TITLES
Nicole Kidman *Pam Cook*
Star Studies: A Critical Guide *Martin Shingler*

FORTHCOMING
Brigitte Bardot *Ginette Vincendeau*
Sabu *Michael Lawrence*

Elizabeth TAYLOR

SUSAN SMITH

A BFI book published by Palgrave Macmillan

First published in 2012 by
PALGRAVE MACMILLAN

on behalf of the

BRITISH FILM INSTITUTE
21 Stephen Street, London W1T 1LN
www.bfi.org.uk

There's more to discover about film and television through the BFI. Our world-renowned archive, cinemas, festivals, films, publications and learning resources are here to inspire you.

Palgrave Macmillan in the UK is an imprint of Macmillan Publishers Limited, registered in England, company number 785998, of Houndmills, Basingstoke, Hampshire RG21 6XS. Palgrave Macmillan in the US is a division of St Martin's Press LLC, 175 Fifth Avenue, New York, NY 10010. Palgrave Macmillan is the global academic imprint of the above companies and has companies and representatives throughout the world. Palgrave® and Macmillan® are registered trademarks in the United States, the United Kingdom, Europe and other countries.

Designed by couch
Cover images: (front) *Suddenly, Last Summer* (Joseph L. Mankiewicz, 1960), © Horizon Pictures Ltd; (back) *The Sandpiper* (Vincente Minelli, 1965), Metro-Goldwyn-Mayer/Venice Productions/Filmways

Set by Cambrian Typesetters, Camberley, Surrey
Printed in China

This book is printed on paper suitable for recycling and made from fully managed and sustained forest sources. Logging, pulping and manufacturing processes are expected to conform to the environmental regulations of the country of origin.

British Library Cataloguing-in-Publication Data
A catalogue record for this book is available from the British Library
A catalog record for this book is available from the Library of Congress
10 9 8 7 6 5 4 3 2 1
21 20 19 18 17 16 15 14 13 12

ISBN 978–1–84457–486–5 (pb)

(*previous page*) Elizabeth Taylor on the set of
Suddenly, Last Summer (1959)

CONTENTS

ACKNOWLEDGMENTS

I am grateful to the Arts and Humanities Research Council and the University of Sunderland for their support in the completion of this project. Thanks must also go to Elayne Chaplin for covering my teaching so ably while I was on sabbatical. I am indebted as well to all the staff who helped me at the Margaret Herrick Library, Academy of Motion Picture Arts and Sciences in Los Angeles (especially Barbara Hall and Janet Lorenz), the UCLA Film and Television Archive and USC's Warner Bros. Archives. The *Film Stars* series itself would not have happened without the sterling support of the BFI Publishing and Palgrave Macmillan and I am fortunate to have such an excellent co-editor in Martin Shingler. I am grateful for having been given the opportunity to present parts of my research at various events in America, France, Germany and the UK, the feedback from which has been invaluable. Researching Elizabeth Taylor's career has been quite a journey and one that I hope will long continue.

I dedicate this book to my wonderful sister, Julie.

INTRODUCTION

In 1944, Elizabeth Taylor appeared in *National Velvet*, in her first leading role, and was instantly hailed by critics as a major new child star. 'Elizabeth Taylor, playing Velvet, is in every respect of talent, presence and appeal already a star. She is fated for a great name in pictures. No one seeing this picture will forget her vivid charm' proclaimed *Variety* (1944a). The *Hollywood Reporter* similarly praised 'the picture's presentation of a sensational new young star in Elizabeth Taylor', observing that:

The girl, given her great opportunity, reaches the heights. She offers a sweet, appealing characterisation which yet has great power. Likewise, it is a pleasure to note that she does practically all of her own riding, some of it distinctly difficult and spectacular. With this performance, stardom is inevitable for her. (1944b)

Amid these and many other glowing reviews, critic James Agee wrote:

Frankly, I doubt I am qualified to arrive at any sensible assessment of Miss Elizabeth Taylor. Ever since I first saw the child, two or three years ago, in I forget what minor role in what movie, I have been choked with the peculiar sort of adoration I might have felt if we were both in the same grade of primary school. I feel I am obligated to this unpleasant unveiling because it is now my duty to try to review her, in *National Velvet*, in her first major role.

So far as I can see on an exceedingly cloudy day, I wouldn't say she is particularly gifted as an actress. She seems, rather, to turn things off and on, much as she is told, with perhaps a fair amount of natural grace and of a natural-born female's sleep-walking sort of guile, but without much, if any, of an artist's intuition, perception, or resource. She strikes me, however, if I may resort to conservative statement, as being rapturously beautiful. I think she also has a talent, of a sort, in the particular things she can turn on: which are most conspicuously a mock-pastoral kind of simplicity, and two or three speeds of semi-hysterical emotion, such as ecstasy, an odd sort of pre-specific erotic sentience, and the anguish of overstrained hope, imagination and faith. Since these are precisely the things she needs for her role in *National Velvet* – which is a few-toned-scale semi-fairy story about a twelve-year-old girl in love with a horse – and since I think it is the most hopeful business of movies to find the perfect people rather than the perfect artists, I think that she and the picture are wonderful, and I hardly know or care whether she can act or not. (Agee, 2005 [1944], pp. 156–7)

Considered in isolation, Agee's description of Taylor as 'rapturously beautiful' seems emblematic of the celebratory tone that pervaded many of the reviews of the young actress's performance in *National Velvet* at the time of the film's release. Yet while Agee *is* saying, ultimately, that he thinks Taylor *is* 'wonderful', unlike the other reviews listed previously, his is far from a straightforward endorsement, following on as it does from his assessment that: 'I wouldn't say she is particularly gifted as an actress'. Interestingly, the only other critic to express scepticism about Taylor's acting abilities in *National Velvet* does so in similar terms. Thus, in his review, Manny Farber wrote:

Pandro Berman, the producer, and Clarence Brown, the director, have made it into a conservatively exciting and engaging film whose chief virtue is its acting, especially a letter-perfect, beautifully felt performance by Mickey Rooney as the jockey. Miss Taylor seemed to me vaporous, though beautiful, either because she is actually a negative screen personality or is made to seem so alongside a particularly virile, smart group of actors, which includes Rooney, Anne Revere and Donald Crisp (who are her parents), a thin-skinned red horse, which appears to be running faster than any horse I've ever seen in the movies, and the child, Jackie Jenkins, who still seems cut off from this civilization and has been wisely left (as Margaret O'Brien and Skippy Homeier have not been) more child than actor. (Farber in Polito, 2009, p. 216)

Agee and Farber both express other reservations about the film that are occasionally echoed elsewhere but what sets their reviews apart from the rest is their evaluation of Taylor's performance according to this 'beautiful rather than talented' criteria. The latter is most concisely encapsulated in Farber's phrase: 'vaporous, though beautiful' but it is Agee's prefacing of his critique of Taylor as an actress with his confession regarding the unsettling impact made on him by her beauty that is the most complex and revealing. In admitting to this, Agee's review raises the issue of the child star's vulnerability to the adult male spectator's voyeuristic gaze, something that Graham Greene had controversially invoked seven years before when suggesting that there was a less wholesome side to Shirley Temple's audience appeal in his review of her performance in John Ford's *Wee Willie Winkie* (1937) (Greene quoted in Temple Black, 1989, pp. 184–5). This more troubling side to Agee's confession is acknowledged by the critic himself through his reference to it as 'this unpleasant unveiling' although the openness with which he admits to his feelings of adoration for the young actress seems a far cry from the furtive pleasure Greene attributes to Temple's adult male audience. Rather than aligning himself with the controlling position of the male voyeur, moreover, Agee construes himself as a critic whose usual acumen and authority have been seriously undermined and thrown off balance by Taylor's beauty, the honest recognition of which prompts him to begin his review with that remarkable opening disclaimer: 'Frankly, I doubt I am qualified to arrive at any sensible assessment of Miss Elizabeth Taylor ...'.

Given this and his subsequent admission of his critically befogged state – '*So far as I can see on exceedingly cloudy day*, I wouldn't say she is particularly gifted as an actress' – how, then, are we meant to take the stringent critique of Taylor's acting that follows? On the one hand, it's possible to understand it as a triumph of critical objectivity over human weakness, with Agee on this reading to be commended for refusing the temptation to offer her a glowing review simply on account of her beauty. Yet the very extremity of his critique might also lead one to read it as an act of overcompensation motivated by a need to recover his critical authority and control. The disabling effect of Taylor's beauty on Agee acquires another layer of complexity when considered in the light of the preternatural womanliness she exhibited as a child actress. The troubling effect of this on the male observer can be traced right back to the very start of her movie career, finding expression in Universal Pictures' casting director Dan Kelly's purported remark: ' "The kid has nothing. Her eyes are too old; she doesn't have the face of a kid" ' (Hirsch, 1973, p. 23; Walker, 1990, p. 32; Spoto, 1995, p. 30; Taraborrelli, 2006, p. 41). This grown-up aspect to Taylor's appearance is often cited as a reason for her failure at Universal, her brief, unsuccessful stay (which resulted in one minor role in the forgettable comedy short *There's One Born Every Minute* in 1942 when she was ten years old) formally terminated when studio executives decided not to take up the second option on her contract (Walker, 1990, p. 33).

Universal's dismissal of Taylor's star potential on such grounds is heavily ironic given how, as Foster Hirsch observes,

it was those preternatural eyes and that wise face on the body of a child that were to be the making of Elizabeth Taylor. Even as a ten-year-old, Liz radiated the womanly wisdom and instinctive female guile that helped make her a star. (Hirsch, 1973, p. 23)

The comments made by Universal's casting director are nevertheless indicative of how Taylor's appearance challenged comfortable preconceptions of what a child star should look like. As Gaylyn Studlar observes:

Taylor was not a 'cute moppet' in the Temple mold but an unusually beautiful little girl with qualities that might lead us to call her a 'womanly girl' whose womanliness created for Hollywood both a problem and an opportunity. (Studlar, 2010, p. 16).

In arguing that 'the sexual power of the virginal little girl' (ibid.: 29) is more safely contained in Taylor's MGM films than in Twentieth Century-Fox's *Jane Eyre* (1944) where her performance (enhanced by the film's strategies) is more 'erotically charged' (ibid., p. 27), Studlar provides one possible explanation for why Agee makes no mention of this womanly aspect to Taylor in his review. Agee instead prefers to imagine himself as regressing to the state of innocent schoolboy 'choked with the peculiar sort of adoration [he] might have felt if [they] were in the same grade of primary school'. Yet while adapted by director Clarence Brown to the needs of the family film, Taylor's performance in MGM's *National Velvet* nonetheless displays a highly nuanced elaboration on this girl/woman dialectic. This is evident right from the outset during the opening scene at the school when, in a matter of moments, Taylor moves her portrayal of Velvet from that of an enchantingly funny little clown-like figure to introverted dreamer.

It's an effect that owes much to the increasing volatility of the young actress's eyes, which, on being lowered, lifted, then lowered and raised again (in response to the teacher's (Norma Varden) question as to what she 'dream[s] about hour after hour'), perfectly evoke the delicacy of Velvet's emotional condition, as a child hovering on the verge of adolescence. The impression it creates is rather like the opening and closing of a drawbridge into the girl's mind and, as such, it suggests Taylor's skill, even at this early stage in her career, in using her eyes as a way of alerting us to the less knowable aspects of her character's consciousness. It's a moment of performance detail that thus demonstrates how, as Andrew Klevan puts it: 'our disposition towards a narrative is not necessarily tied to our identification with character – however elegantly refined – but lies equally with appreciating the performer's capacities for revealing *and* withholding aspects of the character's sensibility' (2005, p. 9). In advancing this argument, Klevan draws on the work of Stanley Cavell, observing that:

Cavell understands 'privacy' to be a central aspect of Hollywood performance, and in discussing *Now, Voyager* (Irving Rapper, 1942), he writes: 'The wish in the great stars … is a function not of their beauty, such as that may be, but of their power of privacy, of a knowing unknowness. It is a democratic claim for personal freedom. It is something [Bette] Davis shares with the greatest histrionic romantic stars, Garbo and Dietrich, sometimes Ingrid Bergman, and among American women, Barbara Stanwyck' (quoted in Klevan, ibid.).

Taylor's emotionally charged lowering of her eyes during the opening scene in *National Velvet* demonstrates her capacity, too, for suggesting a 'power of privacy … a knowing unknowness'. It's a technique that she would employ throughout her career and in *National Velvet* she does so to rich and varying effect throughout, usually as a way of signalling Velvet's tendency to retreat into an inner world of deep thought at moments of crisis. This culminates in the final scene when she sits at the window with Velvet's mother (Anne Revere) as the latter tries to explain Mi's (Mickey Rooney) reasons for leaving. Rather than turning to face Revere, Taylor continues to look ahead, casting her eyes downwards for most of the time in an act of withholding made all the more moving given the closeness of Velvet's relationship with her mother. Through this now much more prolonged lowering of her eyes, Taylor suggests a heightened need for

privacy in her character, evoking the powerful sense of a young girl suddenly having to come to terms with a wealth of emerging adolescent feelings for her friend. When she does finally turn her head towards Revere and the camera, the effect is all the more overwhelming as we are suddenly confronted with a face overflowing with emotion and a pair of eyes iridescent with tears.

As well as bringing to fruition that tension between child and adolescent states that was first established during the scene at the school, Taylor demonstrates an advanced capacity here for creating a meaningful dialectic between restraint and excess in her performance. Her successful negotiation of this may well owe something to director Clarence Brown, whose sensitive orchestration of these and other tensions in Taylor's performing identity contributes to the creation of several star-defining moments. Consider, for example, the earlier scene in the stable when Taylor first gives voice to Velvet's dreams. On being asked by Mi: 'Have you

ever been quiet for a few hours and just think?' she looks down for a moment, tying the cord on her robe. Then, reaching out with both hands towards a wooden post, she pulls herself towards it before bringing her face to rest at an angle on her hands while sighing softly:

All the time. All the time, about horses. All day and every night. I want to be a famous rider. I should like to hunt, ride to hounds. I should like to race. I should like to have so many horses that I could walk down between the loose boxes and ride what I choose.

Taylor's initial act of pulling herself towards the post in a circular movement is very childlike, recalling her fleeting appearances in *The White Cliffs of Dover* (1944), also directed by Brown, where she is shown swinging bashfully against a fence while speaking to Roddy McDowall's character. But the subsequent image of her that we are greeted with in close-up is much more mature and composed. This is reaffirmed at the end of this scene when, puzzled by Mi's unwillingness to feed the family horse for himself, she walks towards him as he stands leaning moodily against the doorway, and gently asks: 'Mi, why be ashamed of your feelings? If you like Miss Ada, well, why pretend you don't?' 'Because I told you I hated horses' replies Rooney, continuing to stare stubbornly straight ahead. 'You'll have to get over that, Mi'. 'Why?' asks Rooney, now looking at her. 'Because I love them so' says the actress before leaning back herself against an adjacent wooden support. At this, Brown cuts to a concluding close-up of her as she slowly rolls her head back in a resting position. Turning in the direction of the camera, she gazes out into the distance while observing in a hushed whisper: 'Every day I pray to God to give me horses, wonderful horses. To let me be the best rider in England.'

Radiating sincerity and purity of faith, Taylor in one sense encapsulates here what Jane O'Connor argues is the child star's ability to act as a modern-day equivalent of the ancient archetype of the wonder-child or Christ-child (2008, p. 104). There is at the same time, however, a quality of sensuous rapture to her performance that, along with the womanly refinement of her face, seems to elicit from her director the kind of special, dreamy close-up treatment that he more typically reserved for adult female stars like Greta Garbo.[1] The final close-up is especially evocative of this, casting Taylor as it does in that actress's classic romantic pose: face tilted upwards, looking intensely into the distance, the voice lowered to a hushed whisper, the words themselves uttered in the form of a slow, relaxed exhalation that seems to draw out this moment in a manner befitting the gradual unfurling of Velvet's ambitions. Like Garbo, too, Taylor manages to achieve an intimate rapport with the camera, thereby bearing out C. David Heymann's observation (with regard to the young actress's first screen test for *National Velvet*):

The instant Clarence Brown and Pandro Berman viewed the test, they realized that Elizabeth had blossomed into the persona required for her first major film role. 'Something quite magical happened between Elizabeth and the camera,' claimed Brown. 'George Cukor said once that it's the camera who chooses the star. There's no way of knowing in advance whom the camera will love. In *National Velvet*, the camera loved Elizabeth Taylor, and it would love her for decades to come.' (1995, pp. 46–7)

The maturity of Taylor's on-screen presence coupled with her director's Garbo-like treatment of her may well help explain why, in her case, Agee eschews the more habitual approach of praising young ingénue performers for their non-actorly qualities (as, like Farber, he does elsewhere in his review in relation to Jackie Jenkins (2005 [1944], p. 158)) and judges her instead according to the rigorous criteria more typically reserved for seasoned adult actors. Like Farber, Agee makes a particular point of contrasting Taylor's perceived acting deficiencies with Rooney's skilful use of technique, thereby going against the tendency in other reviews to praise her for her ability to hold her own among a 'superlative cast' (Anon., 1944b, 1945). Agee concedes at one point that Taylor has 'a fair amount of natural grace and [somewhat vaguely and with a hint of sexism] a natural-born female's sleep-walking sort of guile' but this isn't enough to offset what he regards as a mechanical quality to her acting arising from her lack of 'an artist's intuition, perception, or resource'. He does go further than Farber in acknowledging her ability to convey 'ecstasy, an odd sort of pre-specific erotic sentience, and the anguish of overstrained hope, imagination and faith'. But in construing these as merely 'two or three speeds of semi-hysterical emotion' that 'she can turn on' at will, he dismisses what is in fact an impressive dramatic range to her performance. In stressing such elements, he also ignores her capacity for subtle restraint – something that Studlar conversely highlights in her account of Taylor's brief but haunting performance in *Jane Eyre*. Referring to the scene (marking the actress's first appearance) where her character Helen returns to the darkened school assembly hall to feed and console the ostracised

Whereas Rooney can be praised for giving a perfect performance that is well-nigh 'unimprovable', Taylor is therefore only accorded the merit of producing a collection of individual 'moments'. But while Agee denies her the achievement of an organic performance, the *sheer number* of moments that he admits to raises the question of how someone with such an allegedly mechanical style of acting could transfix this critic so exclusively on so many occasions. A similar contradiction afflicts Farber's review, which claims at one point that:

Velvet's love for horses is written past the usual insipid movie point for such childhood fanaticism and is made to seem, sometimes painfully, like the real thing. ... Her passion seemed to me at all times more real than Bernadette's [in *The Song of Bernadette* (1943)]. (Farber in Polito, 2009, p. 217)

Given the above assertions, one wonders how such emotional conviction could have been achieved without a compelling performance by the actress playing the part. It's certainly difficult to reconcile Farber's comments here with his earlier indifference to Taylor as a 'vaporous' and 'negative screen personality'. In Agee's case, the implication, given his opening confession, is that it was Taylor's beauty that so compelled his attention. Yet his choice of the word '*piercing*' to describe the impact of such moments doesn't correlate with the notion of Taylor as a passive screen beauty simply there to be looked at and enjoyed for her physical appearance. Indeed, it is, if anything, Agee himself who is immobilised to the point of being transfixed.

In praising Taylor's beauty at the expense of her acting, Agee's review is (with the exception of Farber's) largely untypical of the general critical acclaim that greeted the young actress's performance in *National Velvet* at the time of the film's release. But it is uncannily prophetic of the problems that Taylor would face as she moved into adulthood and her blossoming beauty began to blind studio executives and critics to her potential as an actress. Troubled and troubling, honest and revealing, it offers a fascinating acknowledgement of the male critic's difficulties in responding objectively to Taylor as an actress while at the same time initiating a broader debate concerning the extent of her talents as a performer that would accompany her throughout her career.

In *Acting Hollywood Style*, Hirsch discusses the inhibiting, entrapping effect that the actress's 'almost inhumanly splendid' 'beauty mask' had on her career (1991: 179). Noting how her exceptional face meant that 'expectation of acting prowess is low' and 'condemned her characters to romance as a career' (ibid. 180), he points out that it was only during her final years at MGM that she began to break away from the studio's typecasting of her in roles designed mainly to showcase her beauty, observing of her work 'In *Raintree County* (1957), *Cat on a Hot Tin Roof*, *Suddenly Last Summer*, and *Butterfield 8* (1960)' that:

Though she remains encased in her beauty, she enacts neurotic, unstable characters whose beauty is in fact problematic (a threat or a burden or, surprisingly enough, undesired by the men her characters desire). And she adds a wit and temper that indicate her eagerness to crack through her movie-star façade. (ibid., p. 179)

According to Hirsch, it is only by casting aside her glamorous image in more iconoclastic fashion that she was finally able to give what many regard as her greatest performance: 'In *Who's Afraid of Virginia Woolf?* (1966) she dismantles "Elizabeth Taylor" to become a braying middle-aged housewife who is earthy, bitchy, and fat, and freed from her beauty mask, she acts up a storm' (ibid.). Overall, however, she remains, he argues, ultimately defined and framed by the otherworldly nature of her movie-star beauty: 'A woman with a face like Taylor's was destined to be on the screen, but once there her beauty could refer only to itself, to its own photogenicity.

Inescapably, her face speaks "movie star"' (ibid., pp. 179–80). Hence, while crediting Taylor with some success in overcoming the impediment posed by her striking beauty, Hirsch is actually quite restrained in his assessment of her talent:

Though a performer who looks like the young Taylor isn't expected to do much more than offer herself to be looked at, she often did do more. Despite the fact that, inevitably, her entire career has been conducted under the sign of her beauty, Taylor has sometimes acted well. (ibid., p. 179)

Taylor, for her part, has displayed considerable modesty about the extent of her talents as an actress, once declaring 'Richard's [Richard Burton] a great actor; I'm just a broad' (quoted by Schoenberger, 2011). On accepting the twenty-first American Film Institute Lifetime Achievement Award in front of her peers in 1993, she also confessed: 'I, along with the critics, have never taken myself very seriously. My craft, yes, but as an actress, no' only to then quip 'But I wasn't all that bad, was I?' Her comments elsewhere about how frustrated she became by the limited roles MGM offered her during the pre-*Giant* (1956) stage of her adult career and her striving for more demanding parts[2] do suggest a desire to prove herself as an actress, however. Ridgeway Callow, an assistant director who worked with Taylor on *Rhapsody* (1954) and *Raintree County* (1957) certainly felt that she had immense potential. For him, though, the main impediment to its fulfilment was not the actress's beauty or the studio's typecasting of her on account of that but a trait inherent within her own personality. Thus, in an interview with Rudy Behlmer, he recalls the great fun the crew had with her on the set of *Rhapsody*, before going on to observe:

I really believe that if Liz Taylor had the drive of, say, Bette Davis, she would have been the greatest actress ever in the picture business – including Garbo. I think she had the natural ability, but was just a bit lazy. (Callow, 1976, p. 105)

Taylor's famous desire to live life to the full may well be a factor in accounting for any such lack of 'drive' although for Camille Paglia the potential that Callow identifies was actually fulfilled:

Elizabeth Taylor is, in my opinion, the greatest actress in film history. She instinctively understands the camera and its nonverbal intimacies. Opening her violet eyes, she takes us into the liquid realm of emotion, which she inhabits by Pisces intuition. Richard Burton said that Taylor showed him how to act for the camera. Economy and understatement are essential. At her best, Elizabeth Taylor simply *is*. An electric erotic charge vibrates the space between her face and the lens. It is an extra-sensory pagan phenomenon. (1992, p. 16)

While the extent of Paglia's initial claim is open to debate, there are, as we have already noted, suggestions, even as early as *National Velvet*, of how Taylor 'instinctively understands the camera and its nonverbal intimacies' and how, 'Opening her violet eyes, she takes us into the liquid realm of emotion'. The main merit of Paglia's argument is that she makes clear the filmic criteria by which she is defining the source of Taylor's greatness as a screen performer: one that roots her talent in an understanding of the workings of the camera and the revelation of private feeling it demands. It's a stance that is echoed (albeit without the larger claims to greatness) by Lillian Burns (Sidney), MGM's drama coach from the late 1930s through to the 1950s. On discussing the ways in which film acting is distinct from stage acting, she once observed:

In motion pictures there is a camera, what I have termed a 'truth machine.' You cannot say 'dog' and think 'cat,' because 'meow' will come out if you do. I can say that there are people who are definitive motion picture actors and actresses, but not necessarily great stage performers. Katharine Hepburn happened to be both. Elizabeth Taylor, in my book, is a definitive motion picture actress. She absolutely is in love with the camera, the camera is her lover. That's what she gives to it, and that's what comes through. (Burns Sidney, [1986] 1988, p. 2)

Paglia is not afraid to highlight the downside to such a scenario, commenting that: 'Elizabeth Taylor, it is true, lacks stage training; in live theater, she shrinks' (1992, p. 16).[3] But in suggesting a consummate responsiveness on Taylor's part to the conditions of movie acting, she and, more implicitly, Burns, locate her agency as an actress in those very features (eyes, face) that Hirsch regards as entrapping her in the stereotype of passive screen beauty. As such, they seem more open to the possibility of Taylor being able to express herself as an actress at an earlier stage of her career than Hirsch, whose construal of her beauty as an entrapping mask that must be broken through, leads him to consider this star as only truly realising her full potential at a relatively late stage in her career, once such liberation has been achieved through her iconoclastic performance in *Who's Afraid of Virginia Woolf?* (1966). Hirsch does commend Taylor's acting in *A Place in the Sun* (1951) and *Giant* but attributes much of her achievement there to the guiding hand of director George Stevens. Paglia also cites Taylor's work in *Giant* as one of her 'great performances' but she includes alongside that the one she gave in *Elephant Walk* (1954), a film more usually regarded as one of the low points in the actress's early adult career (1992, p. 17).

In explaining Taylor's talent for intuition in terms of her astrological sign, Paglia, however, makes no attempt to explain what this interpretive mode of response involves while at the same time precluding any discussion of the role played by training and experience in shaping the actress's work. By stressing the visual or 'nonverbal' nature of Taylor's 'mythic power', furthermore, Paglia crucially underplays the vital contribution made by the actress's voice to her performances. She has a point when arguing that: 'Her weakest moments on film are when, as in *Cleopatra*, she pushes her voice for grand effects and ends up sounding shrill' (ibid., p. 16) but, in stressing only its limitations, she overlooks a deeper significance to Taylor's voice that Richard Dyer so ably brings out:

Elizabeth Taylor was indeed a great beauty. All the same, that too is not enough for stardom; it needs to be offset by interest, even cut by something dissonant, the vinegar for the greens. With Elizabeth Taylor it is her voice.

This might not seem to be her greatest asset. It is high, thin, often squeaky or shrill. Most of the great women stars have voices either in a lower register (Garbo, Dietrich, Crawford, Stanwyck) or of an almost preternatural softness (Margaret Sullavan, Marilyn Monroe, Audrey Hepburn). They are voices of balm. Taylor's is nothing like this. Occasionally its tartness seems reined in, and then she seems dull and opaque – for part of what makes Taylor's fascinating performances fascinating is precisely this sharp little voice in that sumptuous body. (1992, p. 113)

Rather than disparaging Taylor's voice as her Achilles heel, Dyer insightfully recognises that it is its very dissonant qualities that, operating in tension with her physical beauty, are vital to the complex nature of her star identity and appeal. Such properties arguably became more accentuated during the mature period of her adult career and, in his defence of Taylor's voice, Hirsch refers to it in more complimentary terms as 'a dry, light, high, sandpapery, lovely instrument' (1973, p. 13) that, in her earlier years, her voice *harmonised* with her physical beauty:

Quite unlike her later Chaucerian persona [he's referring here to the bawdier on-screen image that Taylor projected in films such as *Who's Afraid of Virginia Woolf?* and *The Taming of the Shrew*, 1967], the young star of the forties and early fifties had a sweet and almost otherworldly quality. Her high, breathy, whispery, oddly accented voice (a mixture of British and Beverly Hills), which often throbbed with feeling, together with her violet eyes and chiseled features gave her a radiance unscarred by vulgarity. She had to be cast carefully, as either outsiders or as characters who could pass for 'normal' only within the protected realm of studio-made imitations of life. (1991, p. 179)

Whereas Hirsch regards the extreme beauty of Taylor's face as ultimately bestowing (even post-*Virginia Woolf*) a movie-star remoteness that is distancing and unrelated to reality, Dyer finds in her less-than-perfect voice an instrument that helps explain 'why, at her most memorable, she is so achingly alive' (1992, p. 116):

At times it sounds common and can even lend a cheap, sulky look to her lips. Given her well-to-do English parentage and her frequent casting as a rich girl, this is all the more surprising, and enchanting. Her untouchable, rich-are-different air becomes engaging, sympathetic, not-so-different. ...

The voice adds edge, cutting the blandness of loveliness. It is especially apt to suggest needy desire and its frustration, and also a sense of something indefinable and unnamable about what is desired. The voice carries what may be read into aspects of both her 'private' life and her screen roles. The succession of husbands, the drama of divorce and remarriage often intensified by tragedy (the death of Mike Todd in an air crash), scandal ('stealing' Eddie Fisher away from Debbie Reynolds) and farce (the Burton saga), suggests someone determined to have a good time but also hints that the good time is perhaps never quite found. (ibid., pp. 113, 115)

In making the above point, Dyer draws attention to Taylor's tempestuous off-screen life, the much-documented drama of which, while capable of being read (as he suggests) in ways connected with her voice, has generally served as another major distraction to serious evaluation of her film career. At the height of the actress's fame (or notoriety) in the late 1950s and throughout the 1960s, the sensationalist press coverage of her scandalous affairs with Eddie Fisher and Richard Burton threatened to swamp her on-screen identity almost entirely, rendering objective analysis of her work seemingly impossible. The ongoing fascination with the actress's off-screen celebrity is reflected in the plethora of biographies that continue to be written about her, the last of which, *Furious Love: Elizabeth Taylor, Richard Burton, and the Marriage of the Century* (Kashner and Schoenberger, 2010) is now the subject of a rumoured biopic. This is in marked contrast to a noticeable shortage of academic writing on the movie career of a twice Oscar-winning actress[4] voted the seventh greatest female screen legend by the American Film Institute and widely regarded as one of the major film stars of the twentieth century.

Paglia and Dyer's insightful pieces have gone some way towards redressing this neglect although the brevity of their chapters afford little scope for in-depth analysis of her movie roles and performances. Hirsch's book *Elizabeth Taylor* (1973) constitutes a more sustained attempt to evaluate her film career although the sections on her individual movies, while illuminating up to a point, remain quite brief and there is no detailed reading to speak of. Studlar's essay on Taylor as a child actress is the most sensitive to matters of performance but its exclusive focus on the disruptive potential of her erotically charged on-screen presence leaves other crucial aspects to her early star identity unexplored. Such writing on Taylor has much to commend it but, relative to the longevity of the actress's career (spanning 1942–2001) and the extent of her filmography, it remains an as yet small body of academic scholarship.

While recognising the limits that a volume of this size places on its own study, this book therefore sets out to offer a more in-depth exploration of Elizabeth Taylor's work in film. In so doing, its aim is not to dismiss the wider cultural impact of surely the most vibrantly enduring example of female celebrity in the twentieth century. Rather, it is to ask how might a refocus on Taylor the actress open up fresh ways of understanding her significance as a movie star? The overwhelming preoccupation with her off-screen life over the years strongly justifies – by way of counterbalance – a more concentrated focus here on her film roles and performances. Having said that, the book will highlight how her movie-star persona and celebrity image interact at key points in her career and some of the ways in which the reportage of her 'private' life affected the production and reception of her films. The media obsession with Taylor's turbulent personal life during the 1950s and 60s in particular and the dominant construction of her stardom along these lines (at least prior to the 1990s) has also had the effect of overshadowing her early career as a child performer, the academic neglect of which has been compounded by the marginalisation of the child actor/child star within performance/star studies more broadly. Studlar's work on Taylor offers an important corrective to this and one that this study will complement by examining the vital formative nature of the actress's early career and the influence it has exerted over her later stardom.

The book therefore begins in Chapter 1 by focusing on Taylor's star-defining performance in *National Velvet*, examining the significance of her rapport with the horse in that film and its seminal role in forging her on-screen identity. Chapter 2 moves on to consider how the actress was able to make the difficult transition from child to adult star and, in charting the reemergence and ongoing evolution of her on-screen persona, explores the fascinating but hitherto overlooked ways in which her childhood association with animals and nature feeds into her later films. The second half of the book sets out to understand what makes Taylor so distinctive as a film performer and, in particular, it addresses the widely held perception that she is primarily a very instinctive actress. In interrogating this notion, Chapter 3 considers some of the historical factors that may have contributed to her professional development and, having examined the impact of the working conditions she faced as a child actress at MGM, goes on to explore the importance of her much celebrated but little understood collaboration with Montgomery Clift. In assessing the nature and extent of Clift's influence over her, the book at the same time identifies aspects to

Taylor's acting that cannot be explained in terms of the traditions of performance that he and studio-era practitioners variously drew upon and in the final chapter it moves on to consider the role that compassion plays in her work. By engaging with these aspects, it is hoped that the book will help illuminate the rich significance of a film career all too long eclipsed by the media's preoccupation with the actress's beauty and celebrity and in so doing arrive at a deeper understanding of this complex, dynamic performer and the contribution her on-screen work has made to her enduring stardom.

1 RIDING TO STARDOM

Some of my best leading men have been dogs and horses.

Elizabeth Taylor (quoted in Ursini, 2008, p. 32)

Meeting The Pie

Velvet Brown (Elizabeth Taylor) and her sisters have just broken up from school for the summer holidays and are walking through the village. Having left Malvolia (Juanita Quigley) at the sweet shop, Velvet continues on her way with Edwina (Angela Lansbury). On seeing this oldest sister march imperiously past her boyfriend Ted (Terry Kilburn), deliberately ignoring him, Velvet expresses surprise at her impoliteness only to be gently mocked in return. 'Velvet, you're too young to understand some things. Have you ever really felt keen about anything?' asks Edwina. 'Oh, yes!', replies Taylor's character emphatically, stretching out her left hand towards a horse standing harnessed to a cart nearby. 'Horses!' responds Edwina in disgust, 'What does it feel like to be in love with a horse?' 'I lose my lunch', sighs Velvet. 'You're a child', continues Edwina scathingly and, lifting her right hand up to her heart, she asserts grandly, 'Here's where you feel it. It … it skips a beat.' On watching Edwina depart left of frame for her romantic tryst with Ted at the Spinney, Velvet skips along to a nearby bridge and, bending down, picks a cane of grass from the hedge for use as a makeshift riding crop. Then, turning around gleefully to check that no one is watching, she passes through the open gate that marks the boundaries of the village. With the vivid blue expanse of the sea in the distance, she sets off along a country track, holding her body upright as her legs jump up and down frenetically in pretend horse-like movements, urging her imaginary steed on in excited, high-pitched tones and slapping her stick against her side. The vibrant colours and open reaches of the sea and sky heighten the utopian feeling arising from Velvet's act of breaking free from the ties of family and school life and, as she moves off into the distance, the film dissolves to a shot showing her now at the top of a hill overlooking Sewels, to the left of which sits Mi (Mickey Rooney), resting by the crossroads.

Oblivious to his presence, she continues along the lane, her equine exhortations still audible amid the music, before being brought to a halt by his calling out to her: 'Whoa! ... I wouldn't be cantering that horse uphill' he advises. 'I don't usually. I was hurrying', replies Velvet. 'Hurrying? Where to?' enquires Mi. 'No place. Just hurrying', she says matter-of-factly. A brief exchange between them ensues, during which Velvet's attempts at friendliness and sympathy are met with sarcasm and defensive pride from the impoverished Mi (now alone in the world following the death of his father). Then, just as he begins to soften in his approach on seeing her hurt reaction ('Didn't mean to be rough with you, but a fella gets tired of people being sorry for him. He gets not to like it'), she becomes distracted by the sound of a horse neighing in the background. Turning around, still clutching her makeshift riding crop in both hands, she hurries across towards a stone wall bordering a field, her excitement signalled by the introduction of a dramatic strain of music on the soundtrack. There she is greeted by the thrilling sight of a majestic chestnut-coloured horse galloping freely (without harness or rider) across the pasture, the deep blue sea again iridescent in the background. After him chases Farmer Ede

(Reginald Owen), his shouts of 'Whoa!' audible amid the grand pulsating score, which, mirroring the rhythms of the horse's hooves, perfectly captures the exhilaration of this moment.

And so begins the most important sequence in Elizabeth Taylor's film career: the one that, in paving the way for her first encounter with the horse, would set her on the road to movie stardom. Prior to the film's release, Taylor was not by any means a child star, having played only minor/secondary roles in a small number of films. Looking back at her performance in MGM's *Lassie Come Home* (1943), it's easy to detect in retrospect the presence in fledgling form of her on-screen persona as the beautiful little English girl endowed with a touching compassion for animals. The secondary nature of her role there belies the pivotal place she occupies: like a good little fairy, her acts of kindness towards the beleaguered collie ('Poor Lassie. Poor Lassie. Poor girl') are what drive the narrative towards its satisfying conclusion. But *Lassie Come Home* didn't make Taylor a star. It is only with *National Velvet* that she was able to assume the equivalent of Roddy McDowall's character in that earlier film, moving from her role as kindly onlooker figure to playing the part of the main child whose close bond with her beloved animal forms the centrepiece of the story.

At the time that *National Velvet* was released, it was Mickey Rooney, not Taylor, who was the established star of the picture and this is reflected in the decision by director Clarence Brown and screenwriters Theodore Reeves and Helen Deutsch to depart from Enid Bagnold's source novel (2000 [1935]))[1] by structuring the film's narrative around his character's journey to and from the village of Sewels. As well as granting Mi's emotional journey a greater weighting than in the book, this foregrounding of Rooney's star presence posed a potential challenge to the primacy of Velvet's relationship with her horse. Such a threat is evident in the staging of her first encounter with this animal since, in timing it so that it follows on directly from her initial meeting with Mi, it invites

Velvet's passionate response to the horse to be read, in psychoanalytic terms, as a displacement of her emerging feelings of attraction towards Rooney's character. That this scene should even be amenable to such a reading is in one sense quite daring, countering, as it does, the conservative strategies that Studlar argues the film employs so as to contain and defuse the more radical implications arising from 'Taylor's erotically charged feminine presence' as a child actress (2010, p. 32).[2] This potential romantic subtext is suggested by other elements in the script, most notably Velvet's naming of the horse The Pie (which rhymes, of course, with Mi)[3] and her appropriation of Edwina's words (both here and elsewhere) to describe the horse's emotional impact on her. 'It's like Edwina said. It skipped a beat instead of losing lunch', she enthuses softly while holding her right hand up to her heart as Lansbury had done earlier. But as a means of understanding the full complexities of Velvet's relationship with the horse and the latter's importance in forging Taylor's stardom this kind of reading is quite limited, bearing some resemblance to those biographical accounts of the actress that construe her love of animals purely as a substitute for/precursor to her romantic relationships with the opposite sex[4] (more on which in Chapter 4).

To interpret Velvet's passionate response to The Pie purely as a displacement of her attraction to Rooney's character would in fact be to impose on her relationship with the horse an anthropocentric viewpoint (particularly a psychoanalytic reading of the horse as 'phallus') that is out of kilter with Taylor's performance. On talking to the horse, as she befriends it in the lane, the actress perfectly encapsulates what Freud construes as the child's non-arrogant way of relating to animals.[5] Lowering her voice so that it assumes a deeper, throatier sound (like a horse's welcoming nicker), she soothes the animal in a manner quite at odds with the farmer's malign interpretation of him: 'There. What a lovely boy he is. Oh, you're a sweet one', she says on approaching the horse and reaching up towards him. Then, on being told by Ede that the gelding is 'a murderous pirate not deserving of a name!', she protests by bestowing on this creature an identity that the farmer steadfastly refuses: 'Oh, no, not "Pirate". He's a gentle one. I'll just call him Pie.'

During the scene as a whole, moreover, the actress invests Velvet's reactions to The Pie with such emotional intensity that it becomes difficult not to be convinced that she is indeed very *genuinely* distracted by the horse whose exhilarating gallop across the field not only prompts her to interrupt her conversation with Mi but even brings her to the point of losing awareness of him altogether. Her invocation of Edwina's words is thus addressed to herself rather than towards him and when Mi asks her if she is feeling all right (as he does later on in the stable), she expresses surprise on being brought out of this state of self-absorbed wonder, her body trembling in excitement as she tries to explain her reaction to the horse in more understandable terms. 'Oh! Isn't he beautiful? He's new. I've never seen him before', she says with a look of exhilaration on her face.

In her discussion of Velvet's attraction to the horse, Studlar argues that 'The film (like the book) … justifies an excessiveness that could be read as sexual by making Velvet part of a family of obsessive collectors and strivers: her brother collects insects; one sister, canaries; and the other, boyfriends' (2010: 30). The screenwriters' decision to reconfigure the Brown family so that only one daughter is mad about horses allows for a much greater concentration of emotional energy in Velvet, however, than those of the other characters. Their alternative interests (as Lansbury's mock-theatrical display of being in love suggests) are treated as comic infatuations or endearing eccentricities far removed from the grand passion with which Taylor realises her protagonist's equine obsession (all of which ironically undercut Edwina's sense of superiority about her romantic feelings for Ted).

The emotional *excess* that characterises Taylor's performance of such equine passion is strikingly at odds, in fact, with the very notions of *disavowal* and *containment* that underpin an interpretation of her character's love of The Pie as a safe outlet for her desire for Mi. The actress's intense rendering of Velvet's attraction to The Pie instead imbues the girl's rapport with the horse with a sense of value *in its own right*. This in turn raises the question of whether her relationship with this animal can be understood purely in terms of sublimated or displaced sexuality since there are parallels gestured at between them that lie outside such an explanatory framework. It is these aspects to Velvet's bond with her horse that are not catered for by Studlar's reading. In focusing only on how the film seeks to defuse any sexual undercurrent to the girl's passion for 'all things "horsey"' (ibid.), it invokes as its reference point the very same psychoanalytic construction of this animal that was inherent in that earlier interpretation of Velvet's initial encounter with The Pie:

Unlike Alfred Hitchcock's *Marnie* (1962) [sic], which takes the 'horse equals phallus' element of the girl's horse fantasy to its psychosexual limits, *National Velvet* constructs the girl's love of horses as both a phase ('all things in their time,' as her mother says) and the positive psychological impetus for striving for greatness. (ibid.)

Liz Burke also cites Hitchcock's *Marnie* (1964) in her discussion of *National Velvet* but, while this is again for the purpose of contrast rather than comparison, in her case she does so in a way that is much less chained to a psychosexual reading. Observing that: 'It is a text full of fantasy and identification that isn't afraid to represent the overwhelming passion some adolescent girls feel for horses' and that 'Liz Taylor's performance equally embodies that passion to an almost hysterical degree', she argues that, while this 'could be seen as a precursor to the hypnotic stare she uses to bewitch Montgomery Clift in *A Place in the Sun* (1951), a mere six years later', 'the passion here is more innocent, more aligned with fantasies of freedom and autonomy than in her subsequent roles':

A key scene in the film occurs through a transition. We see Velvet in the bedroom she shares with her two sisters, pretending to ride The Pie using string looped through her toes, for reins. The scene dissolves to her riding The Pie in reality, lost in the speed and the feeling of total communication with an animal of another species. (How do I know this? Because I know that feeling.) In the background is a rear-projected scene of sky and sea. There is an element of fantasy here. It is the first time we've seen her on a horse and until this point it hasn't been clear if she even knows how to ride. Visually, it recalls a scene in Hitchcock's *Marnie* (1964), where Tippi Hedren rides her favourite horse. But there is none of Hitchcock's psychosexual weirdness here, just sheer, unadulterated joy. (2002)

This gels more strongly with my own sense that Velvet's affinity with the horse is ultimately founded on kinship rather than notions of sublimated or displaced sexuality. The sequence leading up to her first encounter with The Pie is an important case in point since, in showing her breaking free from the boundaries of the village and riding her imaginary horse along the track, it prefigures the animal's own act of racing across the field then leaping over the wall before galloping down the lane whence she has just come. Her own act of *cantering* her imaginary horse along the lane is crucial in forging this parallel between herself and The Pie since it presents her (like those later sequences of her riding in bed) as both rider *and* horse, human *and* animal, with the top half of her body fulfilling the former role and her legs the latter. Mi's act of shouting out 'Whoa!' to her as she passes him along the lane develops this ambiguous blurring of human and animal identities, invoking as it does a form of exhortation usually addressed to horse rather than rider. It is indeed this very same word that Farmer Ede shouts out to The Pie as he races away from him in the field and this continuity between girl and

horse is reflected in the echoing rhythms of the music as it seeks to
evoke first her 'canter' then his faster gallop. Her description of
herself as going 'No place. Just hurrying' also links *her* more closely
to the wild abandoned movements of the horse than Mi, whose own
earlier purposeful walk along the lane towards Sewels, suggested
(in ways consistent with his character's psychological containment)
a much more controlled, regulated form of behaviour. This is
developed through the pair's contrasting reactions to the sight of the
horse leaping over the wall, with Mi's horrified 'He's loose!' finding
its antithesis in Velvet's excited 'He made it! Did you see him take
that fence?' This pattern of association continues with Velvet's daring
act of running out in front of The Pie, prompting Mi to call out
fearfully: 'Come back! You'll get trampled on!' As Taylor and the
horse come together for the first time in the same frame (with the aid
of back projection), the film presents them like mirror images of each
other. Stretching out her arms while shouting 'Whoa! Whoa! Whoa!'

ecstatically, she prompts him to rear up and spread his forelegs in a rhyming gesture. This rapport between them is also registered at the level of colour through the echoes in her red dress with its white collar and cuffs of his chestnut coat and white markings.

Given such parallels[6] and taking into account the fact that Velvet's second encounter with The Pie again culminates in the thrill of seeing him jump over the wall of the field where he is kept, it's possible to understand her attraction to this horse as rooted in an identification with his wild, rebellious spirit and yearning to break free from the confines of his position. Unlike the earlier reading, therefore, which centred on Rooney's character as the key to understanding that relationship, this one arises out of sensitivity to the creative implications of Taylor's own performance and the affinity it suggests with this animal. As such, it provides a much stronger basis for understanding why the actress's rapport with the horse in *National Velvet* was to prove so crucial to the forging of her on-screen star identity.

Taylor's identification with the animal's desire for freedom first found expression in *Lassie Come Home* during the sequence where her character, Priscilla, is shown deliberately opening the gates of her grandfather's estate in Scotland, thereby allowing Lassie to escape from her cruel mistreatment at the hands of the dog trainer and begin her long journey back home: 'She's going towards south, Grandfather! She's going towards Yorkshire!' cried Priscilla then in exhilaration. In addition to his habit of leaping over the wall of the field (like Lassie's repeated jumping over the cage of her pen), The Pie's impulse to escape from his human bondage manifests itself in his refusal to comply with Velvet's father's (Donald Crisp) attempt to make him earn his keep by working as a farmhorse (following her winning of the animal at the raffle). On being harnessed to the farm cart by Mi on Mr Brown's instruction (despite resistance from Velvet), he proceeds to run amok and cut loose from his bonds, destroying the cart in the process.

The braces motif

This revolt against the farmer's authority invites comparison with Velvet's own later act of gender rebellion in disguising herself as a male jockey in order to race her horse in the Grand National. That central aspect to Bagnold's story must have resonated strongly with Clarence Brown, given his interest in portraying strong-willed women chafing against the destructive constraints of social convention, most notably in *Anna Karenina* (1935). His exciting staging of the race at Aintree certainly makes the most of the moment in *National Velvet* where the young girl's defiance of gender conventions is realised. But such an inclination on her part is insightfully alluded to throughout due to a recurring play on Velvet's resistance to the orthodontic braces that her father makes her wear on her top row of teeth. Studlar interprets the 'reiterated business involving her retainer for her bite' as one of the means by which the film de-eroticises Taylor by emphasising her childishness (2010, p. 31). The more subversive implications of this device become clear, however, when one considers the comparison it invites with the controlling metal bit that is placed in a horse's mouth. It's an aspect to Velvet's character that has its roots in Bagnold's novel although its significance is developed much more fully and coherently in the movie. This begins with the opening scene in the schoolroom when Velvet is shown reacting to Malvolia's observation that: 'She's absent minded. She's always dreaming' and the teacher's question as to what she dreams about 'hour after hour' by pressing her right forefinger and thumb against her top lip in restless agitation. Her troubled response is rendered with exquisite sensitivity by Taylor and immediately establishes a contrast between the prolific, creative world of Velvet's imagination and the constraining effect of the brace. As such, this appliance comes to signify not just a physical pressure on the young girl's teeth but a metaphorical holding back of the free expression and fulfilment of her dreams.

On returning home with Mi (following their first encounter with The Pie), Velvet's attempt to remove her braces at dinner that evening is met with the following telling rebuke by her father: 'How many times must I tell you girls that you have only your faces for your fortunes?' Such a reminder alludes, of course, to the teeth-straightening, appearance-enhancing effects of the retainer and, following on so soon from Mr Brown's contrasting assessment of his son, Donald (Jackie Jenkins): 'That child will make a lawyer', the comment underlines his adherence to the traditional aspiration for his daughters to be beautiful (as the sole determinant of female social advancement and self-worth). Velvet's complaint moments before: 'It aches me when I eat. It's a devil plate!' thus reads as an expression not just of her physical discomfort at having to wear this device but of her unease at the gender pressures and constraints it symbolises. That it is Elizabeth Taylor who plays the role of Velvet invests this moment with considerable complexity. The simple irony, of course, is that the actress is in no need of such a corrective appliance and there is, therefore, a potential incongruity arising from the studio casting her in the part of a character described by Bagnold in her novel as having 'short pale hair, large, protruding teeth, a sweet smile and a mouthful of metal' (2000 [1935], p. 2). The novel's interest in subverting the sexist assumptions inherent in the father's words by having an ordinary-looking girl overcoming all the odds by winning the Grand National is potentially jeopardised, therefore, by MGM's casting of such a beautiful child in the lead role. Taylor's presence risks the film having the contrary effect of reinforcing the father's words, by reassuring audiences of the stunning girl just waiting to emerge once the braces have done their work.

Yet Taylor's performance militates against such a reading. Furtively glancing around the table to see that no one is looking, Velvet pulls the plate out from her mouth only to respond to Edwina's stern calling out of her name by casting a sudden, fearful flash of her eyes in the older actress's direction. The intensity of her stare is like that of a wild animal caught in the act of stealing and this feral quality is heightened by the parallel invited between her stealthy behaviour here and that of the family dog, Jacob, who is shown purloining scraps of food from the table. On hearing Edwina's instruction to 'put that back', Taylor complies but, forcing her eyes open wide and baring her teeth fiercely, she dramatises her character's description of it as 'a devil plate', presenting the image of a beautiful child's face cruelly contorted by its 'satanic' influence. Taylor's response here acquires another dimension when one considers that at the time of making the picture, 'two of her baby teeth were ready to fall out' so 'temporary teeth were painfully rooted in the sockets from which the studio dentist had pulled the baby molars' so as to accommodate the braces (Walker, 1990, p. 44). Given both this and the accounts of how the studio's executives tried unsuccessfully at various points to have the mole on her face removed, her hair lightened and her mouth and eyebrows reshaped

(Heymann, 1995, p. 57; Mann, 2009, p. 81)), such a device becomes additionally symbolic of the external controls that MGM imposed on the young actress herself as it sought to stamp its ownership over her.

Elsewhere, Velvet's attempts to remove her braces occur at moments where the prospect of obtaining temporary release from social restriction and of finding some sort of outward realisation of her dreams is broached. Brimming with excitement at the arrival of Mi (who, as she noted earlier, 'knows all about horses') and the suggestion that his father, Dan Taylor, knew her mother, she slips into Mrs Brown's bedroom on the night of Rooney's arrival only to be checked on putting her hand up to her mouth. Then, on visiting Mi in the stable, having just found out that his father trained her mother to swim the English Channel when she was a young woman, she manages on this occasion to remove her braces and, significantly, it is only moments later that she opens up and gives voice to her dreams about being 'the best rider in England'. The next morning, having persuaded her parents to let her accompany Mi on a delivery (her ulterior motive being to catch another glimpse of the horse *en route* to his destination), Velvet again takes out her retainer just as they approach the field at the top of the hill where The Pie is kept and moments before the animal jumps over the wall for a second time (it's precisely on Mi's utterance of the word 'horse' that this action occurs). On returning home, she attempts to do so once more, this time in excitement at seeing the poster in her father's shop window advertising Farmer Ede's disposal of The Pie via a raffle in the village. Mi checks her on this occasion ('Put your bands back in. Your father's watching') but the import of her action now seems unmistakable. Arising in response to her discovery of this news, it raises hopes in her of owning the horse that are realised later during the sequence where she sits by the front window of the Brown house, recovering from the shock of her ticket not being drawn, only to witness 'the whole village coming here, bringing [her] The Pie'.

That the final instance of this brace removal should occur at the outset of Velvet's journey to Aintree and, hence, at the very point when her dream of entering The Pie in the Grand National is on the verge of realisation provides the ultimate confirmation of its significance. It is preceded, tellingly, by Velvet taking the jockey's clothes out of their box and wondering out loud whether they will fit Taski (Eugene Loring), the rider they have hired to race The Pie at Aintree. The dreamy nature of her musings as she looks over the clothes raises the question of whether her fantasy of racing The Pie herself is in fact already being contemplated by her here. Such a possibility is heightened by her gesture of then running her tongue around her front, top teeth before taking out the retainer and putting it in her handkerchief. On being admonished gently by Rooney's character, she persuades him to relent by pleading (with an exaggeration suggestive of the braces' oppressive symbolism): 'Oh, just this once, Mi. I've got all the rest of my life to wear them!' Given such a coherent pattern of meaning, the braces motif strongly supports a reading that sees Velvet as identifying with The Pie's untameable spirit and longing to escape the human constraints imposed upon him. If one accepts this overall interpretation of Velvet's affinity with the horse, then it's possible to argue that, through her role in *National Velvet*, Elizabeth Taylor's star persona is forged in a way that has strong feminist undercurrents.

Mother and daughter

This dimension to Taylor's persona is also developed through Velvet's relationship with her mother, whose own defiance of social convention by swimming the English Channel as a young woman is parallelled with her daughter's dream of racing The Pie in the Grand National. Their affinity is expressed most movingly of all during the scene when Mrs Brown, on hearing of Velvet's ambition, takes her up into the attic and, opening the trunk containing various mementoes of her Channel victory, gives her daughter the 100 gold sovereigns she won to use as entry money for the Grand National. Taylor's heart-rending cry: 'Oh, Mother! Mother! Mother! We'll win for you, Mother!' tellingly expresses Velvet's kinship with her mother, signifying a promise that is later fulfilled on her return home from Aintree ('Mother, we won'). This explosion of intense feeling finds a dramatic counterpoint, though, in the measured rhythms of Revere's speech. The tension this creates at the level of performance poignantly encapsulates the contrasting states of their two characters: one a young girl still able to give vent to her desires, the other a woman who has long since had to recontain such ambitions on assuming the roles of wife and mother. Thus, on hearing her daughter's declaration, Mrs Brown replies calmly: 'Win or lose, it's all the same. It's how you take it that counts. And knowing when to let go. Knowing when it's over and time to go on to the next thing.' Questioned as to what she means, Mrs Brown explains:

Things come suitable to the time, Velvet. Enjoy each thing, then forget it and go on to the next. There's a time for everything. There's a time for having a horse in the Grand National, being in love, having children. Yes, even for dying. All in proper order at the proper time.

As a commentary on the natural rhythms of life and the importance of recognising that each phase brings with it new priorities and demands, Mrs Brown's speech is extremely moving. But in rationalising Velvet's need to relinquish, in time, her youthful ambitions in this way, her words also efface the social injustices hindering female advancement in society, presenting the losses and suppressions involved as simply part of the natural process of growing up. That Mrs Brown *is* sensitive to the social restrictions preventing female achievement was indicated earlier when she explicitly likened Velvet's dream of winning the Grand National to her own defiance of convention by swimming the Channel. Yet even here the feminist import of her words is qualified by her construal of such moments of rebellion as a sign of some universal impulse towards human eccentricity that everyone is entitled to indulge in on a once-in-a-lifetime basis:

VELVET Often I just sit and wonder about you. I wonder what you're thinking. You don't think like us, mother. You think back here [Velvet points to the back of her head].

MRS BROWN I've seen you do the same. We're alike. I too believe that everyone should have a chance at a breathtaking piece of folly once in his life. I was twenty when they said a woman couldn't swim the Channel. You're twelve. You think a horse of yours can win the Grand National. Your dream has come early. But remember, Velvet, it'll have to last you all the rest of your life.

It's possible to understand this universalising tendency as a means by which this stoical woman has sought to come to terms with the realities of social oppression. But it can also be considered symptomatic of broader containing strategies at work within the family film. The use of Mi's walk to and from Sewels as a narrative framing device is another possible example of this and within the dialogue the containment of such gender rebellion manifests itself in a recurring emphasis on the figure of the male mentor as author of the female's ambitions. In the case of Mrs Brown's defiance of convention in swimming the English Channel as a young woman, she can be heard explaining away the significance of such achievements during her earlier exchange with Velvet in her bedroom. On that occasion, she attributed her success to the motivational impact of her trainer – Mi's father, Dan Taylor, who, as she puts it, 'told me what to do. Worked with me for months. Followed me in a boat. Leaned over and fed me. Breathed the spirit into me.' This Pygmalion-like notion of the man breathing the spirit into the woman is something that Velvet herself invokes when trying to persuade Mi to ride The Pie at Aintree (following her rejection of Taski on account of his heart not being in it). On hearing a distraught Mi berate himself for being 'all soft and yellow inside' and 'no good' to her when she 'needs[s] him most' (due to an earlier traumatic experience he suffered as a jockey), she consoles him by saying: 'No. No, Mi! It's you kept me going. *You breathed the spirit into me. There's greatness* in you, Mi.'

Velvet's emulation of her mother's words here is understandable, given her attempt to shore up Mi's shattered ego and, like her earlier invocation of Edwina's romantic rhetoric to describe her feelings for The Pie, it's not something that can simply be accepted at face value. Mi's response 'There's nothing in me!' directly afterwards offers one such challenge to Velvet's words but they are undercut more completely by a repeated emphasis on *her spirit* as the driving force within the narrative. During her first encounter with The Pie, Farmer Ede remarks: 'You're a *plucky* one, Velvet' on seeing her run in front of his horse and successfully bring him to a stop. 'I like the *spirit* that makes her want to go out after sitting up all night' says her mother to Mr Brown on witnessing an elated Velvet rush out to school following her horse's recovery from illness. It's also Velvet who secretly sends off a letter requesting the entry rules for the Grand National competition (much to Mi's disapproval when he finds out) and she then goes against his advice in broaching the topic with her mother. Add to this the references by Mrs Brown and Mi to how Velvet is 'all lighted up' (during the scenes where it's confirmed that she has won The Pie and when she reveals her dream of her horse winning the Grand National respectively) and we are left in no doubt that she is governed by a strong spirit that resides naturally within her. Her claim that Mi 'breathed the spirit into [her]' is countered, above all, by her decision to ride The Pie herself at Aintree – a feat of daring she has to persuade Rooney's character to go along with. That Mi is first shown finding the resolve to race the horse himself, only to return to the trailer and find Velvet lying asleep, already dressed in Taski's jockey clothes, is crucial in highlighting the strength of her own courage and ambition. Indeed, as the following exchange makes clear, in insisting on riding the horse herself, she does so in full knowledge that there is no necessity for her to do so:

MI   Velvet, I'm going to ask you a question now and I want you to think it over before you answer me. Suppose I told you now that I ... I found a rider.

VELVET   I should still want to ride myself. Mi, I know you're angry but you'll understand. If you ever rode a horse again, you'd want to win. That's how I feel!

MI   So now it's the glory of winning you want for yourself, is that it? [She nods]. You want to ride your race, take your risks and win. You want to win over them all in sight of the world: Velvet Brown before the King and Queen, is that it? [She nods again.]

While Mi eventually accedes to Velvet's wishes, his anxieties about such a venture lead him to admit shortly afterwards (in a further undercutting of both his and his father's mentor status): 'I wish your mother were here.' This subversion of the Pygmalion discourse finds its purest expression, though, in Velvet's own reply to Mi's admission. Gazing straight ahead, her eyes filled with emotion, she whispers: 'She *is* here. [Then, pointing to her chest.] She's *inside* me.' Countering her earlier claim that it was Mi who 'breathed the spirit into' her, Velvet's testimony to the presence of her mother's guiding spirit is invested with immense conviction by Taylor, who delivers this line with a quiet intensity that is deeply moving. This subtler register to Taylor's performance is easy to overlook amid the emotional excess of her performance elsewhere but it's vital in drawing out some of the film's finer shades of meaning and deeper subtexts. During the attic scene, for example,

her sensitive enquiry about the figure in the scrapbook that Mrs Brown is looking at so intently ('Dan Taylor? … You thought a heap of him, didn't you, Mother?') conveys a wealth of insight into Mrs Brown's deeper feelings for Mi's father. The tenderness of her voice as she utters these questions goes far beyond the older woman's prosaic description of her relationship to Dan Taylor ('My trainer'), delicately teasing out from Revere's character's rapt contemplation of this image intimations of a lost/unspoken love for Mi's father while at the same time imparting a deep respect on Velvet's part for her mother's privacy. Taylor's ability to catch the more complex undertones to Revere's performance is suggested above all by her reaction to being reminded that Velvet's Grand National adventure will 'have to last [her] all the rest of [her] life'. Eschewing the temptation to introduce more exaggerated mannerisms into her performance, Taylor simply nods her head slowly while maintaining an intense, knowing look of concentration in her luminous eyes. It's a response that confirms that capacity for deep thought that Mrs Brown had earlier detected in her daughter and, through these actresses' lingering exchange of looks, one senses a much stronger realm of feminist feeling being silently contemplated here.

Fame

These two strands to Taylor's star persona – Velvet's affinity with her mother, her rapport with The Pie – find mutual fulfilment through the young girl's success at Aintree but they interact more complexly during the scene where she returns home and is presented with the opportunity to go to Hollywood. The episode begins with Mr Brown excitedly recounting to his wife the financial opportunities arising from the publicity surrounding his daughter's Grand National escapade only for Mrs Brown, unimpressed (like her counterpart in Bagnold's novel) by fame and the idea of 'making too much money too quick', to suggest: 'We could let Velvet decide.' Her display of faith in her daughter movingly reaffirms the bond of understanding expressed earlier between them in the attic and, in responding to Mr Brown's incredulous reaction: 'Let a child make such an important decision?' with: 'It's in her to do the right', she sets the scene for an encounter that demonstrates, *par excellence*, Taylor's distinctive qualities as a child actress and the richly significant ways in which her star identity is articulated in *National Velvet*.

Responding to Mrs Brown's call, Velvet comes downstairs and joins her parents at the table. The moral alliance between mother and daughter is dramatised by the configuration of the three actors here: Taylor stands near to the seated Revere while Crisp faces them from the opposite end of the table in a gender formation reinforced by the ensuing pattern of alternating shots from over Revere and Crisp's shoulders. On discovering from her father that Hollywood wants her *and* The Pie, Velvet is initially seduced by the prospect. Rolling her eyes upwards to right of frame, she sighs dreamily: 'It might be fun for us to go and see me doing things in the pictures' before glancing towards Mrs Brown and adding: 'Donald would love it!' Turning away from her mother and looking straight ahead again, her expression suddenly changes to one of alarm, however, as she exclaims: 'But The Pie!' Fixing her gaze back on her father, she continues to think things through while Mrs Brown listens intently, her head tilted slightly in the young girl's direction: 'He wouldn't understand. Oh no, he's better here, safe in the fields' she concludes, shaking her head decisively. 'What's the good of that?' asks Mr Brown anxiously. 'You didn't run the National alone. They want the horse too.'

On hearing this, Velvet enquires quietly: 'To stare at? Do they want me to pretend he's a human and knows how to be funny?' Eschewing the temptation to make her voice louder and more strident, Taylor softens it so as to amplify the moral impact and authority of Velvet's words all the more, suggesting the incredulousness of a girl earnestly struggling to comprehend why the adult world would want to treat a horse in such a way. A trace of sarcasm breaks through in the ironic stress she places ever so delicately on the word 'funny', the effect of which is reinforced by a subtle intensification of her stare. Turning to Mrs Brown, Velvet then asks, 'Is that it, Mother?' only for the older woman to look up and say: 'It's your father talking to you, Velvet.' 'Is that it, Father?' asks Velvet (now looking back at Mr Brown), her question delivered in the same quiet, calm voice by Taylor. At this point, the camera adopts a longer view of all three as Mr Brown gets up from his chair and moves towards Velvet. Bending over her, he asks: 'If a horse and rider does something that's never been done before [then, wagging his finger] is it strange or wicked for people to want to stare or [pointing again] newspapers to want to write?' This is followed by a transition to a closer view of father and daughter only as Velvet (in a sudden shift by Taylor to a more intense performance register) blurts out:

But I can't drag him about for people to *stare at*! If you could see what he *did* for me! He *burst* himself for me! And when I asked him, he *burst* himself *more*! And when I asked him again, he *doubled* it!

The acute distress provoked in Velvet by her father's insistent demands comes through in Taylor's delivery of the first line as her lips, moist with emotion, endow each utterance of the letters 'b' and 'p' with a slightly blubbering quality, making the words as a whole swell and lap together in a sea of grief-stricken emotion. Her first utterance of the word 'burst' erupts in a concentrated explosion of feeling. Injecting as much emotion into it as she possibly can and raising the pitch of her voice so that it reaches a crisis point of intensity midway through, she pushes the word itself almost to bursting point in an attempt to convey the extreme devotion she pays homage to in the horse: 'He b*uuurr*st himself for me!' This continues throughout this stretch of dialogue as the rising emotional pitch of Taylor's voice and the accelerating pace of her delivery seek to reenact the immensity of the horse's efforts in leaping and racing ever faster over the fences. The passionate commitment Velvet attributes to The Pie is thus reciprocated in the actress's own emotional expenditure here, thereby affirming, at the level of performance, the strength of bond between girl and horse. Mr Brown responds to this outpouring of emotion by turning away: staring straight ahead, he rocks himself on his heels in agitation, as if to suggest a man literally knocked off balance by the force of feeling unleashed in his daughter. Taylor maintains the moral pressure by keeping her eyes fixed unflinchingly on Crisp, her intense *staring* at *him* forcing his character to experience something of the oppressive nature of what she refers to in the horse's fate.

Bending over his daughter, Mr Brown's attempt to appropriate her words only serves to highlight the crude commercial opportunism of the father who, prior to Velvet's success at Aintree, had shown little support or interest in The Pie, viewing the animal

merely as an encumbrance. 'And would it burst your own foolish heart to stare at an account of five thousand pounds in a solid bank?' he asks in exasperation, thumping his fist twice down on the table for emphasis. Through the pained expression in her eyes and the stress wracked across her face, the actress registers Velvet's extreme distress at the dilemma now facing her, caught as she is between this pressure from her father and her sense of loyalty to The Pie. Staring straight at Crisp, Taylor slowly lowers her eyes and head, signalling Velvet's retreat once more into an inner world of deep thought that on this occasion enables her to discover the moral assurance needed to defy her father. After a brief pause, the actress lifts her head and at this the director cuts to a memorable close-up of her face, now lit with a purity and sincerity of feeling that, along with her shorn hair, endows her with a saintly Joan of Arc[7] quality. Looking upwards intently at Mr Brown, her wide-open, earnest eyes glistening with tears, she cries out in a voice turbulent with emotion: 'I can't help it, Father. I'd sooner have that horse happy than go to heaven!' before clamping her mouth defiantly shut.

The self-sacrificing nature of this decision is underlined moments later when, on turning away to go upstairs, Velvet is asked by her mother about her braces. Looking surprised for a moment, she retrieves them from a handkerchief tucked away in the breastpocket of her suit. Fixing them back on her teeth, she looks up at Mrs Brown and, tilting her head slightly to one side and raising her eyebrows, confirms her dutiful completion of this task by opening her mouth and flashing a wry, forced smile in the older woman's direction. Taylor performs this action with a wonderful sense of irony that suggests a deep insight into its significance for her character, reversing, as it does, the liberating nature of Velvet's earlier removal of this device during her train journey to Aintree. The actress's beauty gives her sardonic humour an added edge, suggesting the acuity of one all too familiar with those expectations of smiling loveliness that she satirises here. Rather like the vaudeville tramp whose blacked-out teeth subvert the traditional expectation of the pearly-white smile, she exploits the unsightliness of Velvet's brace so as to mock the very feminine ideal her wearing of it is meant to achieve. The large frilly collar and ruffle of the orange blouse that she wears during this scene accentuate our sense of Velvet's discomfort at her situation. Jarring with the delicate features of Taylor's face and boyish haircut, it highlights the awkwardness of her character's transition from rebel girl jockey to conventional female, the extravagance of its 'feminine' design even suggesting something of the suffocating effect this return to domesticity entails. That it is Velvet's mother who on this occasion asks her to reapply her braces heightens the poignancy of this moment all the more, given her previous investment in her daughter's dreams. Considered, however, in relation to the constraining nature of her earlier speech – in delimiting Velvet's ambitions to just 'a breathtaking piece of folly' that will 'have to last [her] all the rest of

[her] life' – Mrs Brown's prompting of her daughter nonetheless acquires a deeper logic.

In the final scene, Velvet's mother seeks to console her daughter about Mi's departure by referring back to this moment where she turns down the chance to go to Hollywood, citing her daughter's rejection of these offers of fame and fortune as evidence of her ability to recognise that that part of her life is over 'and *it was time* to go on to the next thing' (a speech that explicitly draws on the one previously made by Revere in the attic). Yet while the mother's point of view is much valued as a source of wisdom within the film and one that is constantly shown unseating the father's attempts to assert his authority, Taylor's moving performance *during* this penultimate scene invites us to read Velvet's rejection of the telegram offers not as a sign of her growing up but as proof of her steadfast adherence to her principled values as a child. It is her concern for the horse's well-being and her democratic belief in their relationship as one based on reciprocal respect and trust that motivate her decision.

Retrospectively, Velvet's rejection of the chance to go to Hollywood on account of The Pie appears, on one level, highly ironic, given that Elizabeth Taylor herself went on to become a major child star as a direct result of her association with the horse in *National Velvet*. MGM certainly sought to capitalise on this association through its promotion of its young actress as 'Nature Girl' and the official fan-magazine literature produced about Taylor following the film's release is dominated by accounts of her 'magical' rapport with King Charles, the horse who played The Pie, along with her friendship with her mare, Betty, which she rode back in England as a young child. This overwhelming emphasis on the young actress's bond with the wild, rebellious horse that only she can handle was quite risky, ideologically speaking, but the articles manage this by promoting her in ways that conform to conventional constructions of the child star. Their persistent emphasis on her spiritual qualities and mystical communion with God is particularly consistent with the Christ-child archetype that Jane O'Connor argues underpins classical Hollywood's portrayal of the child star (2008). This is accompanied by a filtering out of the more subversive aspects to her affinity with the horse, her character's act of gender rebellion at Aintree being an absolutely crucial facet to her on-screen persona that, like Velvet's relationship with her mother and Mi, is never referred to. Contradictions occasionally do arise, most notably when celebrating the pagan nature of her appearance and her egalitarian relationship with animals. 'She resembles a dryad, with her even sensitive features, luxuriant blackish-brown hair, long black lashes and level brows that frame her eyes' says Maxine Arnold in a *Photoplay* article entitled 'Velvet Girl' (1945, p. 34) while the actress herself is cited as saying 'You see horses are just like people. You've got to love them and trust them' (ibid., p. 36).[8] If the latter presents the actress's affinity with nature in ways that are at odds with the anthropocentrism inherent in the Christian religion, then another *Photoplay* article, 'Little Queen Bess', seeks to efface this by comparing Taylor with St Francis of Assisi (Howe, 1945, p. 99).[9] Overall, though, the fan literature on Taylor during her *National Velvet* phase illustrates the dangers of relying solely, as O'Connor does, on extra-filmic media writing for proof of the cultural significance of the child star. Even where the actress conveys a childlike purity of outlook within the film – as during the scene where she rejects the corrupting temptations of fame and fortune for the sake of the horse – she demonstrates how the cultural power of the child archetype can be revivified meaningfully through the act of performance, in this case by challenging adult assumptions about humans' innate rights of dominion over nature.

Velvet's defiant stance against her father acquires added significance when one considers that *National Velvet* was made at a time in 1944 when horses and other animals had been thrust once again into the field of human warfare. It's also set approximately ten years after the end of World War I, a conflict that resulted in an estimated 8 million horses dying on all sides in the service of human conflict (Cooper in Gardiner, 2006, p. 7). In celebrating the special rapport between Velvet and The Pie and construing the Grand National as a route to wish fulfilment, the film could be accused of romanticising, in typical Hollywood fashion, our relationships with animals in a manner that obscures these grimmer realities. Yet, in orienting its overall narrative around Velvet's attraction to the high-spirited gelding that revolts against his servitude to human society and in vindicating her refusal to agree to his exploitation at the end, the film arguably works, in other respects, as an implied fantasy of rebellion against the oppression of horses in wartime.[10]

That Taylor went on to appear in *Courage of Lassie* (1946) must also be borne in mind since, in showing her collie Bill's traumatic experience of being sent to work as a messenger dog for the US Army fighting against the Japanese in the Aleutian Islands in 1942, that movie provides a rare instance of Hollywood acknowledging the valuable role that animals played in wartime and the stresses endured by them in the service of human conflict. Given such privileging of the collie's wartime experience (following his road accident and separation from Taylor's character, Kathie, midway through the narrative), it's perhaps unsurprising, therefore, that it was *National Velvet* and not *Courage of Lassie* that made Taylor a star. In making her relationship with the horse absolutely central throughout, that earlier film doesn't go anything like as far as this one in granting the animal an independent status and subjectivity in its own right. In *Courage of Lassie* the dog is even accorded a brief flashback during his return home from war and Taylor is displaced from the centre of the narrative for significant stretches of the story. Even when Bill returns home, she is not given the degree of prominence that she has in *National Velvet* and one only has to compare the scene where Velvet stands up to her father's pressure for her and The Pie to go to Hollywood with the one where Kathie is forced to rely on her friend Harry MacBain's (Frank Morgan) defence of the dog in the courtroom for evidence of this.

Courage of Lassie therefore highlights, in extreme form, the inherent challenge that the child's empathy with animals poses to the anthropocentrism of Western narratives and movie stardom. In her book *The Child in Film: Tears, Fears and Fairy Tales*, Karen Lury examines the significance of the pairing of children with animals in film, arguing that it tends to reinforce cultural assumptions regarding the former's non-actorly qualities and their status as liminal figures 'perceived as not quite, or not yet, human' (2010, p. 167). But, rather tellingly, she draws from independent, low-budget films rather than child-star vehicles to demonstrate her argument that: 'Some of the most interesting and provocative performances from children in films address or explore how the child is able to 'pass' between the (inhuman) animal and the human' (ibid.).

That the performance of this child/animal affinity is incompatible, in certain crucial respects, with the individualistic

Kathie with Bill during the dog's trial in
Courage of Lassie (1946)

demands of movie stardom might help explain why – despite
Hollywood's known penchant then (as now) for placing children in
animal-centred narratives – it figures surprisingly little (at least in any
deep, meaningful sense) in the construction of on-screen child
stardom. According to William J. Mann, MGM modelled its
publicity for Taylor on Twentieth Century-Fox's 'phenomenally
successful' promotion of Shirley Temple's 'public image around her
love of animals' (2009, p. 72). Such marketing emphasis is not
reflected in Temple's films, however, where her association with
animals rarely carries much weight, if any at all. Even in those where
she is placed in natural settings conducive to its development, as in
Heidi (1937) and *Rebecca of Sunnybrook Farm* (1938), her encounters
with animals tend to be there purely for superficial plot effect and/or

for the purposes of sentimentally reinforcing her cuteness and innocence as a child. One child actor who did excel in expressing an intensely close bond with an animal on screen during the studio era is Claude Jarman Jr. But in spite of his critically acclaimed performance as the young boy devoted to his orphaned fawn in *The Yearling* (interestingly, another Clarence Brown-directed picture made in 1946), unlike Taylor he was unable to make the transition to child star despite MGM's attempts to make this happen. The only other significant child star of that era to develop a strong on-screen association with animals is Roddy McDowall. By the time he appeared with Taylor in *Lassie Come Home*, however, he was already a seasoned teenage actor of fifteen, having previously established himself as a child star through a series of non-animal-centred films. He also starred in two of the other famous horse-centred movies of that period – *My Friend Flicka* (1943) and *Thunderhead: Son of Flicka* (1944) – but he was unable to find in such roles the kind of lasting, multilayered star persona that Taylor did through her performance as the horse-loving girl in *National Velvet*.

That Taylor managed to forge her child stardom in a way that *was* fundamentally rooted in this affinity with animals owes much to her distinctive qualities as a movie actress. Through her consummate skill for expressing compassion on screen and her capacity for bringing a feral intensity to her roles, she was able to assert her on-screen identity in ways that embraced and assimilated (rather than destroyed) this identification with the non-human Other. That it was *National Velvet* and not *Courage of Lassie* that made Taylor a star can therefore be explained not just by the fact that she is more consistently present in the former but by the greater scope such on-screen time gave her to express these key aspects to her performing identity. Even in Taylor's case there are conflicts to be negotiated, however, and, indeed, it's no coincidence perhaps that the moment in the stable where the actress is first granted the exclusive movie-star treatment should also be the one where she gives voice to Velvet's more individualistic ambitions. Although still defined in terms of the young girl's love of horses, her words are now marked by a constant stress throughout on the acquisitional/aspirational first person 'I' and the assertion of a more hierarchical human/animal world order:

I want to be a famous rider. I should like to hunt, ride to hounds. I should like to race. I should like to have so many horses that I could walk down between the loose boxes and ride what I choose!

Once Velvet wins The Pie in the village raffle and the idea of entering him in the Grand National takes hold, there is also a differing emphasis placed at various points on her ambition to win the race for herself and her mother on the one hand and her desire to do it for the sake of The Pie on the other. This contradiction is negotiated through the film's rhetorical play on the braces motif, which coherently roots the young girl's ambition, like the horse's rebellious spirit, in a frustration at the restrictions imposed by patriarchal/human society. This interlinking of girl and horse's shared desire for freedom is summed up by Velvet the night before the race when she offers Mi the following justification as to why she should be the one to ride The Pie at Aintree: 'But he'll be an enchanted horse with invisible wings to take him over every jump if *I* ride him!'

Once the race is over, though, and she returns home, the inability of this motif to reconcile Velvet's human- and animal-centred concerns any longer is made clear by her reapplication of the retainer in response to her mother's prompt. Viewed purely in terms of Velvet's own situation, this is an ominous moment, marking the point where she has to recontain her ambitions and submit to her gender destiny. Yet there is at the same time something extremely noble about the way she now uses her female strength of spirit in the horse's interests, protecting him in a manner that entails a rejection of the anthropomorphising tendencies of cinema itself ('Do they

want me to pretend he's a *human* and knows how to be *funny?*').
That the film reserves its ultimate iconic close-up of Taylor for this
moment where Velvet stands up to her father thus means that the
actress's on-screen stardom is defined here not according to notions
of human ambition, competition or rivalry but in terms of a
profound identification with the animal Other's oppressed position.
That Velvet's anxiety for The Pie's well-being is centred around a
discomfort at the idea of him being *stared* at acquires a special
resonance, given how Taylor herself would go on to become the
object of the media's unrelenting gaze, defined by her beauty and
often deprived of more challenging acting roles on account of this.
As Burke observes:

When considering Liz Taylor's subsequent career, there is a sad irony to her
youthful expression of these worthy sentiments. Here is an actress more
acknowledged for her celebrity than her actual performances. Taylor is
someone who has been stared at all her life. … (2002)

If anything, such hindsight strengthens this scene's self-critique of
Hollywood all the more, endowing Velvet's identification with The
Pie and its relevance to Taylor's star identity with a significance that
resonates well beyond the fictional limits of the film's narrative.
While Taylor's rapid physical development in the years following on
from *National Velvet* would force MGM to jettison her 'nature girl'
image (Walker, 1990, pp. 56–8), prompting the studio to cast her in
parts that, as in *Conspirator* (1950), seemed well beyond her actual
years, as the following chapter will reveal, the actress never really
outgrew her on-screen affinity with animals and nature. Indeed, her
ability to reassert herself as a major adult star is inextricably bound
up with a complex resurfacing of this association from the mid-1950s
onwards.

2 THE ANIMAL RETURNS

Texan rancher Jordan 'Bick' Benedict (Rock Hudson) has just
arrived in Maryland, Virginia during the opening scene of *Giant*
(1956). Having watched through the window as a succession of
riders and their horses race alongside his train as it cuts through the
pasture-land, he is met at the station by Dr Lynnton (Paul Fix) and
they set off in the older man's car. Halting at one point to take in
the sight of a group of riders leaping over a fence, they and the film
audience are greeted by the image of Elizabeth Taylor emerging from
the jump on a magnificent black stallion. 'There he is', says Dr
Lynnton, referring to the horse belonging to Taylor's character,
Leslie, that Jordan has come to buy, 'There's the stallion. That's War
Winds.' At this point, we are granted a closer view of the radiantly
smiling actress as she turns the horse towards them. A cut back to
the two men catches Jordan's initial reaction: 'Beautiful', says
Hudson slowly in rapt contemplation of the image before him at
which Dr Lynnton explains: 'That's my daughter riding him. Leslie.'
On seeing her wave goodbye then ride off to rejoin the hunt, the
father, unsure that Jordan has registered what he has said, reiterates
with growing perplexity in his voice: 'Leslie's my daughter. She's
riding him.' After another pause, Hudson, still unable to avert his
eyes, replies: 'Doctor, that sure is a beautiful animal.'

Considering Taylor's star-defining performance as the horse-
loving young girl in *National Velvet*, her role in *Giant* as the

accomplished New England horsewoman Leslie seems a piece of perfect casting. It's a part that would transform her career, gaining her greater recognition as a serious actress and finally allowing her to take on the kind of substantial, challenging roles previously denied by the studio's casting of her in films largely designed to showcase her beauty. Equally vital, *Giant* enabled Taylor to forge her adult star *persona* in ways that reasserted her on-screen identity as the feisty, independent-minded yet compassionate female and the fact that she enters the film riding the black stallion War Winds is indicative of how this rediscovery is integrally linked to a resurfacing of her association with the high-spirited horse. The affinity between them is underscored by the echoing of War Winds' black shiny coat and mane in Taylor's black flowing hair and riding habit, bearing out Marilyn Ann Moss's observation that: 'She and the horse are interlocked in their beauty, power and wildness' (2004, p. 226). That it's a stallion not a gelding that Taylor is now associated with does make her affinity with the horse much more erotically charged than in *National Velvet*, however, and, in showing her controlling this majestic animal as Hudson looks on, it partly presages her character's strength in handling the strong-willed Jordan. Yet the parallels invited between Taylor and War Winds primarily associate *her* (as in *National Velvet*) with the horse, thereby subverting once more conventional notions of this animal as a symbol of male virility by suggesting a still untamed aspect to the actress's own on-screen image.

Given the above, it comes as something of a surprise to learn that the actress was not first choice for the role, the director George Stevens having initially thought her too youthful to play a character who was required to age twenty-five years during the course of the picture. Audrey Hepburn, Eva Marie Saint and Grace Kelly were consequently all considered before Taylor, whose cause was further hindered by her appearance in a string of largely unremarkable films following her initial breakthrough as an adult star in Stevens's highly acclaimed *A Place in the Sun*. Apparently, it was only the actress's persistent appeals to the director that finally convinced him to give her the part. To what extent Taylor's persona as the horse-loving Velvet started to figure creatively in Stevens's mind and those of his screenwriters once she was cast is not clear but it's interesting to note that the first script to be produced after her casting was confirmed dispenses with the flashback used in the initial story screenplay. That had followed the novel more closely by beginning the narrative with Leslie and Jordan now in their fifties, preparing to fly to Jett Rink's (James Dean) party in Dallas along with their guests and looking back nostalgically on their first meeting in Virginia. The decision to start instead with Jordan's arrival as a young man in Maryland may have been motivated partly or chiefly by a desire for greater narrative economy. But it also had the effect of orientating the film much more strongly around Taylor's star persona, immediately locating her within a setting more redolent of *National Velvet*.

The opening shots of the riders and horses streaming across the fields seem especially evocative of those moments where the actress rode The Pie across the Sussex downs.[1] Taylor's Leslie even fulfils, on an intertextual level, some of Velvet's girlhood dreams: 'I should like to hunt, ride to hounds.' That it's a hunt that Leslie is participating in does compromise Taylor's childhood association with compassion for animals, however, and this more problematic aspect is also suggested by the greater regulation of the horse's movements as they run in parallel with the trajectory of the train (Taylor too, it should be noted, is now riding side-saddle). This contrasts with the freer galloping of a solitary white horse that can be seen passing through a separate field in the foreground of one of these shots, an image that, unlike the horses in the far distance, is more reminiscent of that first exciting glimpse of The Pie as he raced away from Farmer Ede. Whereas Taylor had previously watched The Pie admiringly from her position looking over the wall of his field, moreover, here she is actually riding War Winds. While this strengthens her affinity with this animal, in framing our first sighting of them from Jordan's desiring gaze, the film invites us to recognise how this star's grown-up status renders her more prone to be objectified (like the animal itself) according to her physical, external qualities.

The threat that Taylor's movement into adulthood poses to her association with the horse and the independence of spirit it signifies[2] is signalled, above all, by the proposed *selling off* of War Winds to Hudson's character, the possible reasons for which are elaborated at dinner. On being asked: 'You're here about the horses, aren't you?' by Leslie's mother (Judith Evelyn), Jordan replies: 'Yes, ma'am. I came here to buy your stallion, War Winds, that is, if your daughter don't mind too much.' Mrs Lynnton's response ('Well, in all likelihood, our Leslie will be leaving us soon in any case') makes clear her indifference about the matter and, in hinting at Leslie's possible marriage to Sir David Karfrey (Rod Taylor), her assumptions regarding what must be relinquished if her daughter is to take such a step. The more pressing question raised by the film, however, is whether Leslie herself does in fact 'mind too much' given her joking intervention moments later:

Mother! Let me sell Mr. Benedict War Winds. I can tell you all his bad points. For one thing he eats too much, doesn't he, Father? But you see, it's either War Winds or me. Something has to go.

Leslie's humorous response to the proposed sale of her horse seems far removed from Velvet's passionate defence of The Pie in *National Velvet*, her first line even going so far as to suggest (in ways that would be unthinkable for Taylor's earlier heroine) a readiness to assist in this process. Yet (as when undercutting the mother's matchmaking designs elsewhere) her words are laden with irony and, following on from Mrs Lynnton's intimations about a possible marriage, Leslie's paralleling of her own situation with that of the horse in the final line suggests how she sees herself too as a kind of commodity or encumbrance to be sold off to the most promising bidder. As such, her words imply an identification with this animal that (as in *National Velvet*) seems rooted in a recognition of her own vulnerability to gender exploitation. That Leslie can be sarcastic about the situation nevertheless suggests a much greater emotional control than anything that Velvet could have mustered under such circumstances, although the brief but fiery glance that she throws in her father's direction on hearing him observe: 'Now, Leslie. You know very well that horse is just too spirited for any woman to ride', points to the possible existence of stronger, suppressed feelings. The rationale that Dr Lynnton gives for selling War Winds is hardly borne out by Leslie's earlier confident handling of the stallion and, as such, it says much about the greater threat posed to patriarchy by the actress's dynamic pairing with this animal in adulthood. Ironically, it is Leslie's affinity with the high-spirited War Winds that first attracts Jordan to her and the complexities arising from this human/animal triangle become clearer the next morning during the sequence where Taylor and Hudson's characters are shown coming together as a couple. Stevens's treatment of this is most striking and, in relying for its power on certain strategies to do with shot composition and editing that are not represented in the final script, it suggests that working with Taylor may well have awakened in him a growing sensitivity to the creative possibilities arising from her childhood association with the horse in *National Velvet*.[3]

Having angered and bewildered Jordan at the breakfast table with her critical views on Texan history, Leslie draws him out by departing slowly and circuitously from the room. Pausing at the side table to pick up a morsel of food then walking past him and halting briefly by the doorway, she exits on seeing him get up, then crosses the hall, turning to check he is following as she reaches the front door. A brief shot taken from outside the house shows Dr Lynnton leaving to get the car and (now back inside) we see Jordan emerging from the breakfast room and walking through the hall, conversing with Mrs Lynnton on the way. A long shot of the grounds ensues, with Leslie in the foreground, her back to the camera, standing at the far end of the stone terrace that leads up to the house. Directly in front of her is the doctor's stationary car while, in the far distance, War Winds can be heard neighing as he canters across the paddock. Shifting to a camera viewpoint now outside looking back at the house, Stevens proceeds to privilege us with a medium shot of the actress as she glances down at the piece of food in her right hand for a moment then looks up and stares keenly out in the horse's direction. At this point, there is a cut to a much closer view of War Winds, too, as he stands in the paddock, his head turned towards the house, looking intently at her. The effect of this pair of shots is quite jolting since amid this developing romance between Leslie and Jordan we are suddenly privileged with a human/animal dynamic that seems to belong to a completely different narrative order. It's a very different structure of looking from the one used to

frame our initial sighting of the young woman on her horse in the opening scene. The objectification of her and the animal from Jordan's desiring male perspective then is replaced here by an equal interplay of gazes that (endowing the animal with an active agency and consciousness of its own) is completely independent of him. Its capacity to recall Taylor's on-screen rapport with The Pie in *National Velvet* makes this moment replete with a power of affect that would not have been possible if another actress had played the role. Indeed, in demonstrating how the exchange of looks between human and animal can be indicative not of 'their alienation' but of a form of communication that is 'more primal and perhaps also telepathic' (Burt, 2002, p. 40–1), it's immensely suggestive of the subversive charge that Taylor's eyes can assume when they invite the animal to return her gaze.

In many respects this is a transitional moment, marking the point at which the actress's identification with the horse is disruptively invoked prior to being supplanted by her character's romance with Jordan. It's a shift that is reflected in the replacement of this human/animal exchange of looks with the one between Taylor and Hudson's characters by the sequence's close, although the latter is not the straightforward, happy interplay of lovestruck gazes to be found in conventional romance. By concluding with Leslie looking away from Jordan rather than with the more conventional emphatic image of two in-love people gazing into each other's eyes, Stevens conveys a sense of the difficult, even troubled nature of this transition for *Giant*'s female protagonist. The directness and immediacy of her earlier exchange with the horse are replaced by a structure of looking marked by ongoing tensions and competing pulls. What both forms of looking do share is a certain enigmatic quality and indeed through their perplexed, almost bewildered stares at each other (echoed in the family members' intervening looks of puzzlement on watching the couple come together through their instinctive gravitation towards War Winds at the paddock). It's as if Leslie and Jordan's own relationship becomes infused with the same mysterious force of nature that characterises Leslie's affinity with the horse.

Stevens continues this unusual treatment of the film's central romance by beginning the ensuing honeymoon sequence on the train with a shot of War Winds standing in one of the compartments before panning left to show the two leads looking out of the window in the one right next to him. The pleasure we are invited to feel at this confirmation of the couple's whirlwind romance and marriage is thus mixed with relief that it has managed to avert the threatened parting of Leslie from her horse. Such a moving affirmation of this equine bond is immeasurably enriched by Taylor's star presence but it's complicated by Stevens's ominous superimposition (via a dissolve) of the Benedict family's Reata ranch insignia over War Winds' head as he stands alone in his compartment.

The potential threat this marriage poses to Leslie's own sense of selfhood is vividly suggested by her journey from the lush, green landscape of Virginia (so evocative of the English rural setting of *National Velvet*) to the arid, windswept desert of Texas. The starkness of this opposition was hinted at earlier during the couple's post-dinner encounter on the veranda of the Lynntons' house when Stevens framed the actress by a pillar clad in ivy, its vibrant green leaves encircling and partially concealing her face, while Hudson is positioned next to one bare and unadorned. The grand isolation of the Reata ranch emblematises how Leslie's move to Texas involves her being cut adrift culturally from everything that she is familiar with, her entry into this world forcing her to confront racist and sexist attitudes completely at odds with her more liberal Eastern mentality. This aspect to *Giant*'s story invites strong parallels with *Elephant Walk*, an earlier Taylor film that suffered very different critical fortunes from Stevens's movie but actually anticipates the latter in important ways. That the actress was brought in at the last minute to replace Vivien Leigh, who experienced a nervous breakdown during filming of *Elephant Walk*, has often been cited as evidence that she

was less suited to the role of the complex young Englishwoman, Ruth, who leaves her comfortable existence in a London suburb to go and live with her husband on a tea plantation in Ceylon. But such a view overlooks a deeper logic arising from the casting of Taylor in a narrative centred upon the struggle by a herd of elephants to reclaim an ancient watering trail taken away from them by her character's dead father-in-law, Tom Wiley. That the actress's childhood association with animals in fact made her ideally suited to such a production is borne out by archival records, which suggest that producer Irving Asher originally wanted Taylor to play Ruth but was thwarted in this aim by the news that she was expecting her second child (Heymann, 1995, pp. 120–1; Chapman and Cull, 2009, p. 74).

The parallels between the two films are quite striking. In both, Taylor plays a young woman who falls in love with a man she hardly knows and, following a whirlwind romance, marries and goes off to live with him in a far-off place (dominated by an imposing house) that brings out a darker side to him. Each thereby displays its roots in Gothic melodrama (*Elephant Walk* is particularly indebted to Du Maurier's *Rebecca*) and, combining this with the imperial adventure film and Western respectively, they use their generic hybridity in the service of a critique of patriarchal power and white imperialism. In both narratives, moreover, it is Taylor who acts as the moral centre and progressive catalyst for change. In *Giant*, Leslie's challenging of her husband's values begins even before her journey to Texas, unlike Ruth, who only discovers the truth about the Wiley tea plantation on her arrival there. The basic similarity between these two Taylor protagonists becomes clear, however, when one considers how Leslie's suggestion to Jordan that 'We really stole Texas, didn't we Mr Benedict? I mean away from Mexico' echoes Ruth's observation (shortly after arriving at the plantation) that the elephants' 'road was taken from them, their right of way.' Ruth's instinctive identification with the elephants' plight becomes increasingly bound up with her own sense of gender oppression as a white woman brought from

Ruth stares uneasily at the gold necklace shortly
after receiving it from her husband

England (like John's mother) to Elephant Walk to produce an heir
for the Wiley dynasty. Rather like Velvet's resistance to wearing the
braces on her teeth, her resentment at her situation finds expression
through her discomfort at the idea of wearing the heavy gold
necklace made up of elephant figures that, first given by Tom Wiley
to his wife and intended to be passed down to all future mistresses of
Elephant Walk, is presented to her by John on the night of the annual
festival held in honour of his father's memory.

Like Ruth, Leslie begins to question her husband's values
immediately on arriving at Reata and, given the oppressive
traditions that the house represents, it's apt that Stevens should
stage the couple's first altercation on the porch just before entering
it. Taken aback by Jordan's chiding of her for making 'a fuss over'
the ranch's Mexican workers, Leslie responds to his assertion:

'You're a Texan now' by asking: 'Is that a state of mind? I'm still myself.' Undeterred by his attempt to assert his authority over her ('You're my wife, honey. You're a Benedict'), she insists: 'I still have a mind of my own. Elsewhere, being gracious is acceptable.' That Leslie stands up to Jordan's attempts to impose his racist attitudes on her bears out the significance of the earlier sequence involving War Winds, underlining how she has not lost the strong-willed nature that is embodied in her/Taylor's association with the horse. This is complicated immensely, however, by the sequence following on from the cattle round-up when Luz (Mercedes McCambridge), resentful of Leslie's status as the new mistress of the house that she has presided over since her mother's death (cf. Appuhamy's (Abraham Sofaer) role in *Elephant Walk*) and unable to cope with the idea that an Eastern woman can handle such a stallion, seeks revenge over her sister-in-law by insisting on riding War Winds back to the ranch herself. The episode divides into the following main sections:

1   A jealous Luz arrives at the round-up, driven by Jett in his car. Jordan, concerned at the effects of the heat on his wife, asks Jett to take Leslie back with him. Leslie does so after hugging War Winds goodbye and stroking his forehead and flank.
2   Luz tries to broach her feelings about Leslie with Jordan but he assures her that 'Nobody's setting up against' her.
3   Leslie and Jett engage in conversation as they make their way back in the car, during which Dean's character makes caustic comments about how the Benedicts got to own so much land.
4   Luz insists on riding War Winds herself despite the Mexican worker's warning not to: 'I suppose you came out here to show me how to run things, too,' she growls at the animal. Stevens then shows two excruciating close-ups of her spurs digging into the horse's flank, prompting the animal to neigh in terror and distress as it rides off with her.

5   Leslie and Jett refresh themselves at a roadside water tap. Dean's character starts to open up, telling her how some people (unlike Jordan) do like him and complimenting her on her beauty.

6   Luz is shown in long shot attempting to control the horse, which (neighing distraughtly once again) bucks up and down in protest at her violent treatment of him. Cut to another close-up of the spurs going into his flank.

7   Jett stops the car at the impoverished Mexican workers' village and, on being told by him that some of its occupants are sick, Leslie decides to investigate (thereby going against all her husband's racist prejudices and his family's tradition of not helping these people out). On entering one of the shacks, she encounters a young mother lying in bed while her baby cries in its cot.

8   An injured War Winds arrives back at the ranch without Luz, limping slowly towards the house. Some of the Mexican staff come out to see what is wrong with him.

9   Jett goes into the Mexican woman's house and advises Leslie that they should leave. Leslie tells him that 'This baby is extremely ill' and promises the mother she'll 'be back soon'. Dissolve to a low-level shot with War Winds' head in the foreground as he watches Leslie arrive home with Jett.

In crosscutting between Luz's attempts to subject War Winds to her brutal mastery and Leslie tending to the sick baby, Stevens structures this episode in a way that is clearly designed to bring out the oppositions between these two characters while at the same time suggesting parallels between Luz's mistreatment of the horse and the Benedicts' racist neglect of the Mexicans. That Taylor's stardom is rooted in a compassionate attitude towards nature heightens the contrast between Leslie and Luz all the more although the crosscutting approach refuses any easy continuity between the actress's child and adult personae. By showing how her preoccupation with the sick child renders her completely unaware of the separate trauma involving her horse, it implies, rather, how distant she has become from the animal-centred drama she was associated with as a child and the competing demands now placed on her compassion by the oppressed Mexicans of *Giant*'s narrative world. The follow-on sequence where Leslie returns to the ranch only to discover War Winds injured and her sister-in-law fatally wounded intensifies this all the more. On getting out of the car, a concerned Leslie goes straight to the horse, asking the Mexicans gathered nearby 'What's happened to him?', but on going into the house, she becomes caught up in the human drama unfolding there. Our knowledge of Luz's mistreatment of War Winds prevents us from sharing in Leslie and the other characters' grief at this woman's death and their reading of it as an inexplicable tragedy, prompting instead rival feelings of frustration, distress and indignation at their neglect of the horse's suffering and obliviousness to her culpability. Moral alignment with Leslie is still encouraged due to her decision, just moments after Luz has been confirmed dead, to ask the doctor to go and tend to the sick baby in the Mexican village. Yet, faced with these competing human demands on her attention, we are left wondering even more about the impact of all this on War Winds.

After this scene in the house, Stevens shifts to a view just outside. There, standing alone, holding up his lame foreleg, is the injured War Winds. The music responds with a soaring string motif that movingly evokes the poignant tragedy of his situation. As the horse lifts his head and looks intently in the direction of the door, another shot reveals Leslie emerging from the house and walking towards him. War Winds responds by pushing his head towards her affectionately, as if seeking comfort and reassurance, at which she catches hold of the bridle with her left hand and rubs her other hand up and down his forehead slowly while staring at him pensively only to turn away, seconds later, and move off screen towards the car. Along with the sheer brevity of the encounter, the subdued nature of her reaction comes across as desperately inadequate given our awareness of the severity of War Winds' predicament and the trauma and injustice he has endured. For those sensitive to Taylor's affinity with her horse in *National Velvet*, the poignancy of this brief parting is magnified immeasurably, making it almost unbearably sad. In contrast to the intensity of Velvet's equine passion and constant vocal communication with The Pie, here the actress's muted response suggests almost a hint of censure and disappointment in War Winds for his role in Luz's death, her obliviousness to the injuries that would have revealed his story of victimisation to her betraying a loss of devotion unthinkable in her younger persona.

Significantly, however, the film doesn't simply follow Taylor's character but remains with the horse, the camera's lingering view of him as he stares intently after her rendering *us* acutely sensitive to his unwavering loyalty and attachment towards her and his extreme vulnerability and isolation on being left bereft of the one person whose compassion might save him. In privileging us with this view of War Winds, Stevens disrupts the anthropocentric perspective that holds sway within the Benedict house, gesturing towards another realm of experience more redolent of the animal-centred narratives that Taylor appeared in as a child. It's a moment that recalls, in complex ways, that earlier sequence back at Leslie's parents' home where the horse was shown staring back at her from his position in the paddock. On this occasion, Taylor's Leslie still gazes at War Winds on stroking his forehead but this is conveyed via a medium shot that encompasses both of them in the frame, there being no equivalent of that charged interplay of looks that was so strikingly foregrounded during their earlier encounter. In then withholding any reciprocation of the horse's lingering gaze after the actress as she turns and walks away, Stevens signals a final moment of rupture in her identification with the horse, the point where the mutual recognition and trust that exists between them can no longer be sustained due to the pressure of the other demands placed on her character within the narrative.

Following an elegiac fadeout on this view of the horse, Stevens fades in to a scene later that night in the couple's bedroom. Leslie enters and walks despondently across to the window where Jordan is standing and, as they meet, they put their arms supportively around each other. The camera captures this from a position further back in the room, keeping its distance from the couple as they stand facing the window, their backs to the camera. 'I'm a lot better, honey', says Jordan. 'That's a good boy', responds Leslie, rubbing his back comfortingly. Standing silently for a moment, she continues to stare out of the window only to then ask (with growing apprehension in Taylor's voice): 'Where's – my horse?' After a pause, her husband replies: 'I shot him. Bone was broken. Somebody had to do it. I thought it'd be better if it was me.' In the ensuing silence, Leslie slowly lets her arm drop further down his back while emitting a sad murmur of acknowledgement. 'The baby?' he asks. 'Alive, thanks to Doctor Walker', she quietly replies. At this, Stevens cuts to a closer, sideways view of the couple looking out of the window. It is only now that we are given a glimpse of the actress's face wracked with sorrow and, on hearing Jordan respond to the news of the baby's survival with the word 'Good', she turns and buries her face in his chest.

In having the horse killed off, *Giant* finally enacts what was threatened at one point but averted in *National Velvet* during the scene where The Pie becomes ill with colic and is nursed back to health.[4] Stevens's strategy of privileging us with knowledge of War Winds' trauma encourages us, however, to feel a deep anxiety and unease about what might be lost (or suppressed) in the process of such a change, prompting us to feel a compassionate regard for the animal that we are now much less able to share with the actress

herself. Given the suggestions in *Giant* and *National Velvet* that
Taylor's affinity with the horse is rooted in a shared rebelliousness
of spirit and taking into account also the idea that the stallion in
Stevens's film reflects (unconventionally) a sexual potency in her,
the killing off of War Winds has other potentially troubling
implications. In her biography of George Stevens, Marilyn Ann
Moss actually reads the shooting of War Winds as a symbolic
taming of Taylor's character, arguing that, in order for her to fulfil
her ideological role as domesticator of the Texan landscape, Leslie
has to give up her sexuality in order to become the nurturing

mother: 'The sexuality that led her to Bick in the first place, the signal of her sexuality, War Winds, must be sacrificed.' She goes on to claim that in killing this animal, Hudson's character destroys 'along with it ... any last traces of Leslie's sexual behaviour and appeal. Whereas her sexuality drew Bick to her – and to War Winds – that sexuality has no place in the domestic life Leslie now takes on' (2004, pp. 226–7).

Moss's reading is persuasive up to a point and indeed there is a sense in which the film itself also seems to lose some of its energy and momentum in the post-War Winds section of the narrative. I'm not sure it's quite so straightforward a change as she suggests, however, since Leslie is actually presented at her most sexually alluring during a sequence that takes place shortly *after* the horse's death. This begins with the late-night encounter between the couple in their bedroom when she uses her seductive charms to overcome Jordan's anger at her outspoken criticisms of his male community of friends' sexist attitudes. 'Come on, partner. Why don't you kick off your spurs?' she asks him invitingly as she sits in bed, her face glowing in the darkness. Leslie's success in eliciting the desired response is made clear the next morning through Jordan's thinly veiled suggestion that her energetic love-making has worn him out ('That arguing takes a lot out of me'). Leslie doesn't actually have children at this point so hasn't yet attained the maternal status that Moss argues she assumes in place of her sexuality but she does reveal towards the end of this scene that she is expecting their first child while later on Jett expresses his ongoing attraction to her despite her new role as mother: 'Having kids seems to agree with you, you know? You're looking prettier than ever. Just as good, anyway.' That her 'caveman speech' (during which she ridicules the men's outmoded views) takes place after War Winds' death also complicates the idea that the shooting of this animal constitutes a killing off of her unruly side. Indeed, far from taming this quality in her, it's almost as if the strength of feeling she

had to suppress then now finds outlet in her angry protest against the male regime of Texan society. Hence, on being refused the opportunity to participate in a discussion of politics on account of it being deemed 'Men's stuff', she protests: ' "Men's stuff!" Lord have mercy! Set up my spinning wheel, girls. I'll join the harem section in a minute.' Then, on being pressurised by Jordan to leave, she concludes:

If I may say so before retiring, you gentlemen date back one hundred thousand years. You ought to be wearing leopard skins and carrying clubs. Politics! Business! What is so masculine about a conversation that a woman can't enter into it?

It is in fact Leslie's rebellious stance in this scene that has often been held up as an embodiment of Taylor's progressive persona in

Giant. This is particularly evident in the accounts in recent years that have sought to reevaluate her performance in that role. While the accomplished nature of her acting attracted praise at the time of the film's release, it was largely overshadowed by the posthumous tributes to Dean, who died in a car accident shortly after finishing work on the movie (Taylor was in fact the only one of the three main stars not to be nominated for an Oscar). Commenting on the effectiveness of her 'caveman speech', Thomas Schatz is quoted by Dana Calvo as saying that: 'For two minutes of screen time, that's as powerful a performance and a pre-feminist statement as you'll find in the entire decade of film' (2003, p. E7) while Calvo himself observes: 'There are many women in the Southwest who can deliver a quote or two from Taylor's character, Leslie' (ibid.). Richard Schickel also highlights the actress's performance (unlike Dean's) as a revelation on watching the film again:

> Her incredible beauty (she was 24 at the time) is utterly disarming. But she's full of sass and spunk and cool, effective outrage. She's a premature feminist, refusing to stick to her tatting, insisting on joining the men folk in their glum, scheming talk of politics and business. She's also a humanitarian, determined to lift the Hispanic ranch hands out of their squalor, which she does without once becoming shrill or hectoring about it. Basically she charms all of Reata into righteousness. This is star acting at its best. (ibid., p. 21)

That Taylor is able to assert this feisty side to her persona in the initial post-War Winds phase of the narrative is less surprising if one considers his death as marking a shift in focus from the horse's victimisation to Leslie's own oppression as female Other. In making this transition, *Giant* thus manages to reaffirm, even at the point of separation, an ongoing affinity between Taylor and her horse. This is made clear the morning after her 'caveman speech' when, on hearing Jordan claim –

I run Reata at all times. … That's the way it is. Everything that's in it and on it is run by me. … That's the way it's always been too. Everything that has a Reata brand on it is run by me

– she sits up on the bed and asks indignantly: 'Does that include *me*?!' Leslie's realisation that Jordan regards her, like the animals on his ranch, as subject to his absolute dominion and control links her very precisely to War Winds, whose own subjection to the Benedict rule was signalled by Stevens's symbolic 'branding' of the Reata insignia over the horse's head as the animal embarked (with the newly married couple) on the train journey to Texas. Leslie herself was shown recoiling at the sight of a hot brand being pressed into the hide of a young steer during the cattle round-up and, at the 'welcome' barbecue arranged by the scheming Luz, she faints at the sight of a calf's head being served up. Such revulsion is echoed by her children in the second half of the film when they are shown screaming in distress on discovering that the cooked turkey presented to them at Thanksgiving is none other than the bird they had earlier befriended. Their naming of the bird 'Pedro' gestures (like Stevens's crosscutting during the horse-laming sequence) towards an underlying connection between animals and the Mexican people as oppressed Others in Texan society. This association in Taylor's films not just between herself and animals but between animals and ethnically oppressed people is yet another aspect to *Giant* that hearkens back to *Elephant Walk*.

Overall, the post-War Winds section of *Giant*'s narrative becomes emblematic of Taylor's post-*Giant* career (at least until the mid-1960s) since, from *Raintree County* through to *The V.I.P.s* (1963), the animal itself largely recedes from view only to be replaced in some of these films by an explicit identification on the actress's part with its position as oppressed Other. In *Cat on a Hot Tin Roof* (1957), Taylor actually *becomes* the animal through her persona as Maggie the Cat – a role that Richard Dyer regards as a perfect piece of casting:

She's classy but panicky, sensuous but jumpy with frustrations, like, as she says in reply, a cat on a hot tin roof. Cats are gorgeous creatures, capable of purring but also whining and screeching, adorable but selfish, even adorably selfish. Most of Elizabeth Taylor's performances, on and off screen, hint at this perennial fascination, at once sexually alluring and sympathetically recognizable. (1992, p. 117)

Dyer insightfully recognises the importance of this role in bringing out a key duality in Taylor's on-screen image although whether her Maggie the Cat persona is quite so quintessentially expressive of her star identity as he suggests is open to debate. Instead of the actress's longstanding affinity with the high-spirited, ungovernable horse, here she is associated with a form of animal symbolism that (downplaying cats' own independent streak) is largely defined in terms of sexual frustration, emotional neediness and entrapment. 'I'm not living with you. We occupy the same cage, that's all!' screams Maggie on hearing Brick (Paul Newman) reassert 'the conditions on which [he] agreed to stay on living with [her]'. This pessimistic reworking of the actress's association with animals finds even bleaker expression in *Suddenly, Last Summer*. There, her character, Catherine Holly, is faced with incarceration in a state asylum (Lions View) that is notorious for performing lobotomies on its patients: 'They'll keep me there forever. Like an animal in a cage' she says, echoing her aunt's (Katharine Hepburn) earlier reference to her niece as 'locked in her stateroom like a wild animal'. Taylor's character is also placed in an overall filmic universe in which nature is construed as a hostile, devouring force governed by animals whose rapacious attitude towards other species could not be further removed from the child–animal empathy celebrated in her childhood films. Such a shift can be understood partly in terms of Tennessee Williams's authorial worldview but it also seems expressive of late 1950s America, as the consensus of conformity began to crack and women's frustrations and anxieties at the social constraints placed on them began to surface.

Off screen, Taylor's own life was challenging that façade of female contentment and conformity due to her multiple marriages and divorces and, at the height of the Eddie Fisher scandal, when she was accused by the media of stealing Debbie Reynolds's husband away from her following the tragic death of Mike Todd in a plane crash, her association with animals was, in certain quarters, vehemently turned against her. Thus, when gossip columnist Hedda Hopper penned an article that took issue with Taylor's behaviour, she was inundated with letters from outraged readers protesting at the 'animalistic' nature of the actress's sexuality, some of which drew specifically on her feline persona in *Cat on a Hot Tin Roof*. 'This is the first time I have ever written a form of "fan" letter, but I am so disgusted with Liz Taylor's "alley cat" ethics that I am moved to write' complained one female reader (Anon., 1958a). This can be contrasted with the supportive testimonies that Taylor's more loyal fans offered around this time and, in a piece published in a fan-club newsletter dedicated to the star, one female cites the actress's affinity with animals as proof of her goodness as a person and her possession of a compassionate understanding that the media ironically lacked in its treatment of her:

If only more people would understand Liz as she understands animals, they would realize what a great person she is. In my opinion she is the only actress who can make you believe she is the character she's playing. Elizabeth deserved an Oscar for many of her movies but most of all for 'Raintree County'. If Hollywood doesn't wake up soon they'll lose the best actress they ever had. Let's all of her fans get behind her and make sure she gets what she deserves in the future. (Anon., 1958b)

In *Butterfield 8* (the film that finally secured Taylor her first Oscar), there are signs of a reemerging celebration of the actress's affinity with animals and nature. At one point, a besotted Liggett (Laurence Harvey), having spent the night with her character,

Gloria, is moved to remark that hers is: 'The first genuine wildness I've ever come across in a woman' and, of course, there's that memorable moment where Gloria grinds the heel of one of her shoes into Liggett's foot in defiance of his attempts to master her. Any impulse to endorse this fiery, independent femininity in Gloria is complicated, however, by the film's rooting of her social unconformity in an experience of sexual abuse suffered in childhood, by its predictable killing off of this character in a car accident at the end and by its casting of the actress in a role that some regard as an attempt by MGM to capitalise salaciously on her 'Bad Girl persona' (Mann, 2009, pp. 273–4). This problematic treatment of Taylor is reflected in Gloria's troubled association with the mink coat that she is shown 'borrowing' from Liggett's wife's wardrobe on leaving his apartment in the first scene and which finally brings about the break-up of her relationship with Harvey's character. 'I couldn't go back to thirteen again. I had one chance to stop it! One last chance! And I … I threw it all away for thirty-two animals sewn together in a coat!' she cries in anguish on revealing to her best friend, Steve (Eddie Fisher), what has happened. Taylor's only interaction with a live animal comes in the form of a brief, inconsequential exchange with the friendly Yorkshire terrier (apparently, the actress's own) that resides in Gloria's mother's home.

In *Cleopatra* (1963), Taylor's leading lady makes her grand entrance into Rome seated on a giant sphinx, a mythological creature consisting of a lioness's body and human head. On one level, this figure's hybrid status typifies that blurring of human/animal identities that is such a feature of the actress's star persona. This isn't a live animal, however, but a lifeless stone statue, often used to mark the location of tombs of the ancient pharaohs of Egypt, and, seated impassively on it, Cleopatra becomes a deified object of worship, her immobilised state relieved only by the mischievous wink she casts in Caesar's (Rex Harrison) direction. It's an image that seems indicative of how the glamour and spectacle surrounding the actress's adult stardom had reached a state of such magnitude that they were threatening to drain the life out of her vibrant associations with nature. Viewed in this context, it's rather telling that her only interaction with a live animal in *Cleopatra* comes in the form of the deadly asp that she turns on herself at the end as she takes refuge with her loyal female servants in the pharaohs' tomb. That her performance as the strong female Egyptian ruler was on some level able to resist such stultifying tendencies is suggested, however, by Brendan Gill's famous description of Taylor (who was, after all, playing the Queen of the *Nile*) as 'less an actress by now than a great natural wonder, like Niagara or the Alps' (1963).

It wasn't until *The Sandpiper* (1965) that Taylor's affinity with animals and nature would fully rediscover its positive potential. This film cast her in the role of Laura Reynolds, a free-spirited artist who lives, unmarried, with her son (born out of wedlock) in a cabin by the ocean on the spectacular Californian coastline known as Big Sur. Surrounded by the sandpiper and other marine birds who form the subject of her paintings, Taylor's character revels in the independence she enjoys from conventional society, espousing a feminist politics that bears the influence of Betty Friedan's *The Feminine Mystique* (1963). Despite its considerable box-office success, the film was ridiculed by many critics – whether for exploiting (through its story of a happily married minister who embarks on a passionate affair with Laura) the scandal surrounding Taylor's relationship with Richard Burton, or for miscasting both stars in roles deemed *too far removed* from their celebrity personae (the idea of Taylor, the glamorous movie queen, playing a beatnik character was considered preposterous by some). Either way, these hostile reviews of *The Sandpiper* reveal the extent to which the sensationalist media coverage of Taylor's off-screen life was now colouring and impairing the reception of her work as an actress. Yet if one reframes her role in *The Sandpiper* through the lens of her overall *film* career, it emerges not as a risible piece of miscasting but as a perfect matching of character and star persona, the pleasures arising from which do much to outweigh any plot/dialogue weaknesses (the criticisms of which at the time now seem disproportionate). Within the narrative, various characters frequently voice a desire to tame Laura's unconventional femininity using a range of avian and equine metaphors. The film, however, strongly endorses her anti-establishment outlook (much to certain critics' chagrin), recalibrating her associations with animals and nature according to notions of freedom and flight rather than entrapment. This is emphasised through her caring for the injured baby sandpiper bird and the film's paralleling of her helping him recover the ability to fly with her liberating effect on Burton's character, Edward. In his final sermon, Edward pays testament to this by declaring his newfound belief: 'That only freedom can tame the wild, rebellious, palpitating heart of man. Encagement, never. That life, unfettered, moves towards life. And love to love.'

Having won over the critics through her iconoclastic, Oscar-winning performance in *Who's Afraid of Virginia Woolf?* and her fiery rendition of Katharina in *The Taming of the Shrew* (1967), Taylor would embark on a series of films that attracted yet more hostile reviews. One of these was *Reflections in a Golden Eye* (1967), the controversial screen adaptation of Carson McCullers's novel. Set on a Southern army base and featuring scenes of nudity and voyeurism, it deals with the events leading up to the murder by repressed homosexual officer Major Weldon Penderton (Marlon Brando) of an ordinary enlisted soldier, Private Williams (Robert Forster), a figure he is secretly attracted to but whom (as he finds out) is deeply obsessed with his wife, Leonora (played by Taylor). In a letter to the producer, Ray Stark, journalist Gloria Steinem (who had been hired by Stark to work on the film's script) cited the actress's readiness to take on such a role as evidence of a non-diva-like quality that could be used as one of the angles to promote the film, observing: 'What other movie queen would have – or does now – take such un-Hollywood-like chances with her glamor?' (Steinem, undated, pp. 2–3). In *Saturday Review*, Arthur Knight put it another way:

> She is one of the few stars – many say the *only* star – who is regarded as a true gilt-edged investment. Her presence in a picture is a sure guarantee that audiences will turn out in sufficient quantity to offset even the staggering costs of a *Cleopatra* … . Miss Taylor's two latest efforts, *The Comedians* and *Reflections in a Golden Eye*, seem almost specifically designed to test the loyalty of her public, each in its own way. (Knight, 1967)

If, for this reviewer, *Reflections* seemed intent on 'test[ing] the loyalty of [Taylor's] public', then at the same time it tapped into a core aspect of her appeal, complexly reworking as it does her longstanding on-screen association with the high-spirited horse. The links with *Giant* are especially striking and this fact is highlighted during the scene where Penderton, increasingly frustrated at his wife's sexual infidelity and agonising over his own surfacing feelings for Williams, tries to ride her white stallion Firebird despite his proven lack of horsemanship. The echoes of the scene in *Giant* where Luz tries to ride War Winds are compelling: in both cases, the character who feels most threatened by Taylor engages in a disastrously failed attempt to gain control over her through trying to master her horse. Here, though, it's the husband himself – not the jealous sister – who takes this drastic course of action and this time it's a frantic bid to deny his homosexuality by asserting a virility he otherwise lacks. The parallel invited between Firebird and Leonora (both unruly creatures that Penderton finds impossible to handle) is confirmed by his sobbing threat to kill the horse on being thrown from it, a reaction that echoes the one he vented earlier on seeing Leonora strip off her clothes in front of him and walk around the house. That he actually exacts this punishment on Private Williams at the end underlines the links between all three of these figures and the threat they collectively pose to Penderton's state of emotional denial.

Whereas in *Giant*, Leslie was too distracted by her concern for the Mexican child and her grief-stricken husband to notice the wounds on War Winds that would have alerted her to Luz's cruel brutalisation of him, here Leonora has no such competing demands on her attention. Her initial shock on seeing the condition her husband is in after his fall is quickly replaced by a suspicion that he is not revealing the full truth of what happened and an overriding concern for the welfare of her horse. Disregarding his assurances that Firebird is all right, she visits the horse in his stable, displaying all the singular intensity of focus that Taylor had shown for The Pie in *National Velvet* during the scene where he falls ill with colic. 'Who beat him?' she cries, distraught at Firebird's condition as he lies groaning in agony from his wounds. On hearing the stables sergeant (Gordon Mitchell) comment knowingly: 'Nobody here, ma'am', she makes it clear that she realises the identity of the guilty party in her enraged reply: 'That son of a bitch!' Returning to the house and the party she had arranged, she appears at the doorway of the room where Penderton is standing with a group of fellow officers. Dressed in evening wear and with her hair swept up elegantly into a beehive, she seems a paragon of female beauty. Yet, costumed in a white dress and with a matching shawl stretching across the upper part of her chest and so far up her neck, she also appears like a human extension of Firebird, defiantly declaring her affinity with the stallion whose brutalisation she has come to avenge. It is from this glamorous yet equine image of Leonora that her anger spills forth as she whips Penderton's face repeatedly while screaming through ferociously bared teeth: 'You lousy bastard beating my horse, my Firebird!' One reviewer criticised this scene in the film, arguing that it should not have made literal what Leonora had only threatened in the book, citing it as an example of how 'Things are clumsily spelled out here' (Unsourced, 1967, p. 33). Considered in terms of Taylor's star identity, however, Leonora's whipping of Brando for mistreating Firebird has a

tremendous logic, emphatically reasserting, like a return of the repressed, the primacy of Taylor's childhood identification with the horse.

The feral nature of her acting here reminds us how her on-screen identification with animals expresses itself at the level of performance, not just persona, the full force of which, previously reined in during her MGM years, now finds freer outlet in the less controlled climate of the 60s.[5] It is this aspect to Taylor's performance that prompted the prominent New Zealand playwright Bruce Mason to observe, in a letter he wrote to director John Huston in praise of the film:

As for the acting, I have seldom seen anything to touch it on the screen. ... From this showing Elizabeth Taylor is the world's most under-rated actress (and I am quite sure she won't mind that being said.) No one alive can express, as she can, an almost abstract female cruelty; only fatigue, one surmises, ever extinguishes Lenore's [sic] blazing <u>terribilita</u>; the moment where she throws 'stallion' at Weldon was like a whip. She has the most superb insolence; her slow, almost tender stripping, to an impotent man, was quite bottomless in its savagery. (Mason, 1969)

The incident that Mason refers to is from earlier in the film where Leonora taunts her husband about his lack of heterosexual masculinity by proclaiming 'Firebird is a *stallion!*' If, on that occasion, Taylor's vocal delivery assumed the lashing force of a whip, then this finds its ultimate realisation during the party sequence. Her ability to achieve 'an almost abstract female cruelty' and 'blazing <u>terribilita</u>' in her performance is something that Taylor had first demonstrated in her role as Martha in *Who's Afraid of Virginia Woolf?* – the ferocity of her acting in that film again bearing out the idea that, in the physical absence of the animal itself, she is liable to assume aspects of this identity herself. In both films, the unsettling nature of her performance owes much to Taylor's withdrawal (for the most part) of the compassionate persona that had so defined her earlier work. In *Reflections*, her character's cruel taunting of her husband seems all the more merciless given his inner anguish about his latent homosexuality and, as such, this role complicates any more straightforward continuity in her on-screen identification with human/non-human forms of Otherness. This links it to *Giant* once again, although *Reflections* generally lacks the self-consciousnesss about this issue that made Stevens's movie so insightful as an elegiac meditation on the implications arising from Taylor's transition to adult stardom. That Penderton is a representative of the military elite (and so proud of the status this brings) does make Leonora's hostility towards him characteristic, however, of the ways in which Taylor's identification with animals tends to position her in opposition to white patriarchal authority. Indeed, it is only on seeing his façade of military male control crack during the sequence where he reveals his loneliness and nostalgic longing to be back in the barracks living with the other soldiers that the actress allows Leonora to show traces of an emerging compassion for him.

That Leonora's ferocious whipping of Penderton's face is motivated by her intense concern for the horse's suffering nonetheless crystallises how the feral and compassionate form two distinct yet interrelated sides to this actress's performing identity, both of which have their roots in her performance in *National Velvet*. At a time when the break-up of the studio system, the pressures of Taylor's wider celebrity and the actress's penchant for taking on riskier material were putting all kinds of strain on the coherence of her on-screen identity, this identification with the non-human Other erupts in *Reflections* even stronger than ever. Above all, it underscores her special affinity with the horse, which binds together the three main decades of her film career.

Off screen, Taylor's love of animals has also established itself as a permanent facet of her wider celebrity image, at times achieving a disruptiveness of its own through the various media accounts of how her many different pets have featured in her domestic life, often portrayed as jostling chaotically alongside her marital relationships.[6] MGM's costume designer, Edith Head, paints a vivid image, too, of 'dogs, cats, parakeets, squirrels' and other animals running around while the actress was being fitted for her glamorous, adult, seductive role on the set of *A Place in the Sun* (Head and Calistro, 2008, p. 126). Unlike other female stars like Brigitte Bardot, Doris Day and Tippi Hedren, however, and in contrast to her own tireless humanitarian work championing the fight against AIDS, Taylor hasn't pursued animal-rights activism (as far as I am aware) and, like many actresses of that studio era, her glamour has at times clashed with such values through her occasional wearing of furs. It is in Taylor's films that the more subversive implications of her association with animals find fuller expression and, in providing such a vital source of creative stimulus and sustenance for her on-screen identity for almost a quarter of a century,[7] it is a feature of her work that makes her unique among Hollywood stars. That it should play such an important role in enabling the actress to negotiate the difficult transition from major child to adult stardom is particularly suggestive of her distinctiveness, and, in revealing a profound interrelationship between these two main phases of her work, is indicative of how Taylor's career goes against the tendency within star studies to treat child stardom as a discrete category.

3 ACTING ON INSTINCT?

In the various documentaries, biographies and other material about Elizabeth Taylor, one notion that repeatedly crops up is that she is a very instinctive actress. The insistent praising of Taylor along these lines can be contrasted with approaches within star and performance studies where the term 'instinctive' generally tends to be treated with caution due to its perceived effect of mythologising stars and their performances in ways that ignore the many factors involved in their creation. What we have seen, instead, is the emergence of some notable work by the likes of Cynthia Baron and Sharon Carnicke that counters the film industry's tendency to promote the idea during the studio era that 'film performance was mechanically reproduced instinctive behaviour' (2008, p. 18) by highlighting the training, experience, labour and skill it involved. Building on this important strand of research within performance studies, one of the aims of this chapter is to consider some of the influences that helped shape Taylor's professional development. At the same time, it contemplates the possibility that in Taylor's case there was in fact something genuinely instinctive about her acting, the unconventional nature of which warrants serious attention. In tackling this area, though, it seeks to go beyond habitual definitions of the actress along these lines, arguing that the customary labelling of her as 'instinctive' has all too often served to preclude more detailed consideration of the skills and abilities that she brings to her work.

If this categorising of Taylor as an instinctive actress has become a way of accounting for certain aspects to her approach that are not fully or easily understood, then this invites another fascinating parallel between her and animals, given how, as Erica Fudge has argued, the term 'instinct' is often applied to non-human attributes that are alien and inscrutable to us. Our tendency to judge animals according to a human-centred frame of reference results in a devaluing of 'instinct', she argues, and a denial of the possibility that what we regard as such in animals (e.g. the homing instinct of pigeons) may in fact involve a great deal of intelligence and skill (2002, p. 140). It would be oversimplistic, of course, simply to equate Taylor's instincts as an actress with those deployed by animals since any such attribute in her clearly belongs to the realm of human responses and is thus potentially much less alien and more capable of being understood. Rather than serving as a badge of inferiority, moreover, this quality in her acting has tended to be construed positively, as proof of her potency and uniqueness as a performer. Yet the problems involved in its usage become evident on closer inspection. Consider, for example, Jeanine Basinger's invocation of the term when seeking to explain (in her interview for *Elizabeth Taylor: England's Other Elizabeth*) why Taylor and Montgomery Clift were able to achieve such a moving on-screen rapport:

They're a pair of beautiful people who can welcome the camera up close and who can share their emotional intensity and passion very easily in front of the camera. So he, whatever his training was that gave him access to that kind of thing that he could use as a performance, she had the same access by some kind of natural instinct. (2001)

Basinger astutely points towards an underlying connection in acting terms between these two stars, despite their very different professional backgrounds and, in suggesting that Taylor was able to arrive at a comparable intensity without the kind of formal training that Clift drew on, she compares them in ways that are highly favourable to the actress. The difficulties involved in trying to arrive at a more precise understanding of how Taylor was able to achieve such effects are suggested, however, by Basinger's phrase: 'some form of natural instinct', the vagueness of which only invests the actress's performances with even greater mystique. Spoto similarly invokes the notion of instinctive acting as one explanation for 'why [Taylor's] performances always seemed so unforced, natural and inevitable. They were achieved without self-consciousness, without analysis, without any attempt to vitiate spontaneity by intellection' (1995, p. 56). As proof of the naturalness of this gift, he argues that such a trait was evident even during her childhood years:

When the film rolled, she seemed to turn some kind of inner switch: this instinct, of course, is demanded by the craft of screen acting, which is achieved in small, brief bits and pieces of performance, a moment at a time between the cry of 'Action!' and 'Cut!' (ibid., p. 34)

Anthony Asquith, who directed Taylor much later on in *The V.I.P.s*, also felt impelled to assert that:

Miss Taylor, without question, has a natural, instinctive acting talent. She has an extraordinary sense of rhythm, a quality that cannot be learned. It must be born. The timing of her pauses, her movements, even her facial expressions are instinctively right. (1963, p. 1)

In suggesting that acting came naturally to Taylor, enabling her to respond according to impulses innate to her rather than being something that needed to be learnt, these accounts conform to long-standing notions of instinctive behaviour as meaning 'spontaneous; acting without reasoning, deliberation, instruction or experience; determined by natural impulse or propensity' (Webster, 1828). In his book *Human Instinct: How Our Primeval Impulses Shape Our Modern*

Lives, Robert Winston explains it in terms of 'the distinction between the mind we are born with and the mind that is "made", via learning, culture and socialization' and goes on to say that:

Instinct, then, is essentially that part of our behaviour which is not learned ... . Instinct is those elements of human action, desire, reason and behaviour that are inherited, and those instincts which are specifically human are those that were honed during our time on the savannah. (2002, p. 21)

In basing his argument upon evolutionary theory, Winston's model doesn't explain where *acting* instincts come from nor what they entail but, in arguing that instincts evolve over time, his work is useful in challenging the more romanticised idea that they are simply God-given talents innate within people at an individual level. In going on to qualify the starkness of the opposition he initially presents between learnt and unlearnt parts of human behaviour, his work is also helpful in highlighting the role that environment and culture may play in the development of instinct. Thus, he acknowledges that: 'our environment (and hence our learning) may have a powerful effect on the way our instincts are expressed' (ibid.) and refers to 'the fundamental importance of nurture, experience and the social environment in which we are brought up' (ibid., pp. 34–5). This leads him to argue that: 'Our cognitive mechanisms for dealing with the world – whether they are face recognition, language acquisition or emotional development – will not appear of their own accord. Beyond a certain point, it may be too late to "switch" them on' (ibid., p. 35). Hence, 'Just like the development of a child, the process of evolution is intertwined with the growth of culture, and "culture" began well before evolution finally shaped us as we are today' (ibid.).

This notion that instincts have to develop from somewhere and that they are triggered or shaped by humans' interaction with their environment is a much more complex way of thinking about such forms of behaviour and, interestingly, it surfaces occasionally in some of the discussions of Taylor's acting. Thus, in the same documentary that Basinger appears in, Angela Lansbury begins by stating: 'I think that Elizabeth is an instinctive actress', only to suggest that this was cultivated by contextual factors:

I think she ... was simply brought up around acting. Acting was everywhere in her young life I would have thought. And you do learn so much by watching, listening and viewing, you know, we're all like sponges. (2001)

Similarly, while downplaying the coaching needed to elicit an assured performance from Taylor in *A Place in the Sun*, screenwriter Ivan Moffat nevertheless acknowledges, in the documentary *George Stevens and His Place in the Sun* (2002), how she was intuitively responding to requests made by her director:

Her performance was somewhat of a surprise, how good it was, how natural she was, how good her instincts were, her movements, her turns, her hesitations, all that. She wasn't coached particularly by George in doing all those things. He said what he wanted, and she was very quick to interpret, she was very clever.

In interviews, Taylor repeatedly makes it clear that she regards herself as an instinctive actress who never received any formal coaching but, rather than construing this as some form of preordained, magical talent, she presents it as developing naturally out of her practical interactions with the actors and directors she worked with:

Well all my teachers, because I never had an acting lesson in my life, all my teachers were the people I acted with, that I was directed by, the experience of my life, one on one with people on the set, and that was how I learned whatever was my technique. It was purely instinctive. (ibid.)

This is a very different way of construing instinctive acting from that found in the Hollywood publicity material about stars during the studio era. In exposing the promotional strategies adopted by the industry in this regard, scholars such as Baron and Carnicke have stressed the considerable work that goes into the process of acting. Baron in particular has outlined in detail the inhouse training that emerged in the studios during the 1930s and 40s and notes how dialogue coaches and drama coaches, for example, had become 'an integral – but consistently hidden – part of the process of producing film performances' (Baron, 1999, p. 33). It isn't clear to what extent Taylor was exposed to or influenced by such onsite teachers but, given that: 'The studios ... brought in *drama coaches* to train young contract players and prepare even experienced actors for screen tests and actual performances' (ibid.) and taking into account Lillian Burns's appointment as head of MGM's drama department in 1936 (ibid., p. 34), it seems reasonable to assume that she was not exempt from their advice. Producer Pandro S. Berman relates one such instance during the making of *Ivanhoe* (1952) when Taylor (still recovering from the break-up of her traumatic first marriage and reportedly unhappy with the role assigned to her in the film ((Walker, 1990, pp. 401, 129)) was, apparently, not seeing eye to eye with her director, who felt that he wasn't getting the performance that he wanted out of her. According to Berman, they went ahead and completed the picture in England but, on returning to Hollywood, Taylor was entrusted to Lillian Burns (Sidney) and, with the drama coach's help, the actress's original dialogue was dubbed, Taylor redelivering all of her lines afresh in the studio's looping room (Berman, 1972, p. 107).

As far as I'm aware, Taylor has never publicly expressed her indebtedness to Lillian Burns (Sidney) in the way that actresses such as Janet Leigh (1984) and Debbie Reynolds (1989) – her peers at MGM during this time – have done. Why this should be so is not altogether clear. She may have been following studio practice in not

This photograph offers a rare glimpse of Lillian
Burns (Sidney) coaching Taylor around the
time of *Cynthia* (1947)

Taylor with her mother, Sara, again during the
making of *Cynthia*

drawing attention to the role that drama coaches played in the construction of film performances although, as we have already seen, Taylor was in other respects quite open in acknowledging the impact of 'the people [she] acted with' and 'was directed by' (ibid.). Given the important influence that Taylor's mother, Sara, is perceived to have exerted over her daughter's professional development at that time, it may be the case that Burns simply didn't have the same kind of central role that she did for actresses like Leigh and Reynolds, who often refer to her as a surrogate mother figure. An actress by profession herself, who gave up her own career on the stage when she got married and started a family, Sara Sothern Taylor is acknowledged in all of the major biographies on Elizabeth as a powerful driving force in her daughter's life and early career and Taylor herself has described her mother as 'my best girl friend, my guide, my mentor, my constant companion' (1964, p. 21). Although the biographies tend to interpret Sara's role according to the discourse of the ambitious, interfering, stagestruck mother living out her unfulfilled dreams through her daughter, they are helpful in highlighting her on-the-set coaching of the young actress. Thus, on the subject of *National Velvet*, Walker observes that: 'Mrs Taylor attended the shooting of her daughter's scenes and was observed giving her pre-arranged hand signals – sometimes to Clarence Brown's irritation – to convey the degree of feeling she thought Elizabeth should be showing' (1990, p. 46), while Spoto comments with reference to *Courage of Lassie*:

The production was not facilitated by Sara, who was as usual present, off in a corner of the set but visible to her daughter, whom she coached with an elaborate series of hand signals. If Elizabeth's voice was too high, Sara put her hand on her stomach. If Elizabeth's reading of a line lacked sufficient feeling, she saw her mother put a hand to her heart. If Elizabeth seemed distracted or was not heeding a director's instruction, Sara touched her head with a forefinger. Directors, cameramen and producers were at a loss. According to the contract, Mother was to accompany Daughter to each day's work and was paid to 'assist her in the performances.' Sara knew better than to collide with executives, but there she was, a smiling, affable but somewhat marmoreally imposing figure. And in this capacity she remained for several more years. (1995, pp. 40–1)

If such coaching did take place, then it prompts fresh reconsideration of critic James Agee's observation of the young actress's performance in *National Velvet* – namely, that 'She seems, rather, to turn things off and on, *much as she is told*' (Agee, 2005 [1944], p. 157). If there *is* anything mechanical about Taylor's performance in *National Velvet* (and my own reading of her fluid movement between child and adult, human and animal states suggests something quite the opposite), one might indeed look to this as a potential contributing factor. There is an alternative possibility to contemplate, however, and that is that this system of hand signals may have helped her maintain concentration during rehearsals, providing a means of marking out the various shifts or emotional beats required in her performance so as to ensure that everything was in place by the time that the cameras were ready to roll. In the case of *National Velvet*, this would have been especially important, given the huge leap it involved for Taylor as she moved from minor/secondary parts to major, lead role. That she managed to make this transition so rapidly may well have owed much to her mother's professional guidance and it's all the more notable when one considers the conditions that child actors like herself encountered during that period. In her memoir, Taylor paints a far from idyllic picture of her experience as a child performer at MGM, explaining how, along with her young peers, she was required to move back and forth between her studies at the studio's schoolroom and her acting on set:

I hated my own school because it wasn't a school. The M-G-M classroom was in what used to be Irving Thalberg's bungalow, and I went there from the age

of ten until I graduated. We were required by law to put in three hours a day, so we were doing in that time what normal kids did in six. During a film you'd have a special tutor on the set. So between camera takes you'd cram in ten minutes, twenty minutes of study – going out to act, then being led by the ear back to school and snapping your brain back into being a student. (Taylor, 1964, p. 22)

The stop-start nature of filming that all movie actors are subject to was therefore greatly magnified for the child performer by this constant shuttling back and forth between the roles of school pupil and actor. As well as the confusion such conditions must have posed to Taylor's sense of identity (as she found herself oscillating between being treated as a child and having to take on the professional responsibilities of an adult), they must have placed immense pressure on her powers of concentration as an actress, with her attempts to compose herself for the part, remember her lines and directions all prone to persistent interruption from these other competing demands. Given this, it's perhaps not surprising that Sara Taylor developed a system of hand signals to communicate with her daughter since, as a former stage actress, she must have been especially sensitive to the difficulties entailed in this stop/start style of acting (not to mention the habit of filming out of sequence). Such a mode of working could in fact be cited as another explanation for any tendency towards the mechanical in Taylor's acting in *National Velvet* (she 'seems, rather, *to turn things off and on*, much as she is told') although it's possible that this experience of constant flux between schoolroom and film set may itself have helped to hone that capacity for concentration that the actress would become noted for in her adult career. As Alexander Walker observes: 'Teaching became a series of anticipated interruptions and scheduled dislocations' that 'inevitably produced a special kind of mind: one that could switch, on demand, from arithmetic, geography or English to pouring out emotion in front of the camera as another person' (1990, p. 50).

In her memoir, Taylor attributes her discovery of the art of concentration to a later influence, observing of her collaboration with the actor Montgomery Clift that: 'I watched Monty. I watched how much time he spent on concentration – which has since become the key to my kind of acting, if you can call it acting' (1964, p. 49). Spoto concurs, arguing that:

From Clift, she learned the importance of introspection, the value of joining intuition and spontaneity with a certain interior quiet, so that whatever there was in herself of Angela Vickers [her character in *A Place in the Sun*] could surface immediately from concentration. (Spoto, 1995, p. 64)

The impact that Clift's intense acting style had on Taylor during their first professional collaboration is vividly described by the actress in the documentary *George Stevens and His Place in the Sun*. Observing that it was then that she first 'started to take acting seriously', she goes on to recount her experience of watching him at work:

I thought, 'Wait a minute ... . What's he doing? What's he up to?' And I started to listen and realised that it was more than just 'Cut!' and make some lines you'd learned the night before, hit your mark ... you know ... that it was more than that. That it was something that could make this man shake from head to toe with emotion. And I thought, 'I've got to find out what it is inside him that moves him so completely, emotionally, that can get him to that state as George Eastman, not Montgomery Clift, to make the sweat literally come out on his body, to make his eyes actually fill with tears, as George Eastman.' And I thought, 'What is he doing?' And I began to think about acting, and I would listen to George's direction on a totally different level than I had other directors and began to understand the reasons they had for certain directions. And I think that's when I first began to act.

On the face of it, Taylor's expressions of indebtedness to Clift for turning her into a serious actress could be seen as reinforcing the broader misconception that: 'The Method style that became dominant in the 1950s' was 'based on a progression from an unschooled, instinctive approach to one informed by training and technique' (Baron and Warren, 2011, p. 13). Yet to read Taylor's acknowledgement in this way would be to overlook Clift's own far from straightforward relationship to the Method (at least as popularly construed) not to mention the actress's own deviation in certain key respects from studio-era practice. As Baron and Warren point out, Clift's development as an actor was in fact shaped not by Strasberg but by other important teachers – most notably the Broadway stars Alfred Lunt and Lynn Fontanne as well as his acting coach Mira Rostova, while 'the films that established Clift as a star, *The Search* and *Red River*, had been shot before the Actors Studio opened on October 5, 1947' (ibid., p. 12). Indeed, along with Brando, Clift:

opposed Strasberg's approach, valuing instead what he had learned from people whose reputations were established long before the formation of the Actors Studio. Working with Alfred Lunt and his wife Lynn Fontanne, Clift increased his ability to use script analysis and rehearsals to create 'the thought processes, the specific character needs,' and subtexts that would color each moment of a performance (Bosworth, 1978, p. 77) (Baron and Warren, 2011, p. 11)

Observing that: 'Clift never actively sought membership in the Studio and had left the Studio before Strasberg started teaching in fall 1948', Baron and Warren cite his biographer Patricia Bosworth as saying that: 'Clift "was never truly a Method actor," in that he never used Strasberg's central technique … . From Clift's perspective, a lot of Method actors "never created characters [and] instead merely played variations of themselves"' (ibid., p. 12).

Clift's commitment to creating character rather than 'merely play[ing] variations of [himself]' is something that he learnt from Lunt and Fontanne and is actually closer to the studio-era practitioners' ideas about acting and 'the central principles of Stanislavsky's System' (ibid., p. 8) than the Strasberg school of Method acting. His investment in concentration as the key to effective acting also bore some affinity with standard studio-era practice. As Baron observes elsewhere, 'developing the ability to concentrate … was seen as the basis of convincing performance' by 'acting experts of the period' (1999, p. 42). Above all, it was considered the prerequisite means by which the technique (much advocated in acting manuals) of making mental pictures of a scene so as to bring it (in the words of drama coach Lillian Albertson) *alive in [the actor's] memory* could be achieved (ibid., p. 41). There were, therefore, elements central to Clift's approach that were in harmony with those principles of acting that Taylor would have already encountered growing up in the studio environment and this extended to his commitment (albeit a more extreme one) to exhaustive preparation and extensive rehearsal. But where he offered her something excitingly new was in the very different use to which such skills and techniques were put. As Baron has pointed out, the emphasis on concentration during the studio era was designed to facilitate 'emotional distance from the feelings portrayed' (ibid., p. 42) and both her and Warren cite 'dispassionate execution of performance' (which was designed to protect the actor from becoming too immersed in and drained by the part) as one of the ideas that Lunt and Fontanne shared with studio-era practitioners (2011, p. 8). Yet despite their influence over Clift, it is difficult, from the firsthand accounts that Taylor provides of him in action, to find any evidence of him practising this technique. In her interview for *Elizabeth Taylor: England's Other Elizabeth*, she describes her shock on seeing 'how *involved* he was, his whole being. He could make himself shake and he couldn't stop after the director said "Cut!". He would sweat, real sweat.' She goes on to recall how:

I used to take Monty and say 'Monty! Don't do this to yourself! You've got to release it when the scene's over.' And you know, I'd hold him. I was only sixteen. I think I had my seventeenth[1] working on the film. And it was almost like sometimes I was older than he was. But watching his intensity I learned not to let it kill you but that it wasn't a game. That you had to feel it in your *gut* and your *guts had* to get in an uproar.

It was, then, this sense of becoming the character so completely that one's whole body participates in the experience and the intensity that arose in his performance as a result that seem to have made such an impact on Taylor, prompting her to remark: 'Oh, but there was such energy coming out of him! What was coming out of his eyes and his body. It was, I imagine, like sitting next to an electric chair' (ibid.). In her memoir, she comments on the 'contagious' nature of his style of acting, observing that 'When he would start to shake, I would start to shake' and she describes this giving style of acting as 'almost a physical thing, like an umbilical cord, an electricity that goes back and forth' (1964, p. 49).[2]

While it's important to recognise the impact that Clift had upon Taylor, it may not simply be the case that he taught her this capacity for emotional intensity. As we have seen from an analysis of her performance in *National Velvet*, signs of a tendency towards this style of acting are evident right from the start of her career and we have also identified other possible factors in her early working environment that may have shaped her powers of concentration. In understanding Clift's influence, it may be more accurate to say that, having worked within a studio context that impressed on actors the importance of securing safe emotional distance from character, Taylor suddenly came face to face with someone who offered an exciting alternative that chimed in certain ways with instincts displayed in her own early acting but that may well have been increasingly stifled as she grew up at MGM. The visceral, emotionally much riskier nature of this style of acting is perfectly encapsulated in her observation: 'That you had to feel it in your *gut* and your *guts had* to get in an uproar.'

Although Taylor's collaboration with Clift in *A Place in the Sun* tends to attract the most commentary, it is their final pairing in *Suddenly, Last Summer* that produces the most searching self-examination of their acting chemistry. The self-reflexive nature of this becomes all the more fascinating when considered in relation to director Joseph Mankiewicz's recollections of working with the actress on that picture. Referring to *Suddenly, Last Summer* as 'in every way a gratifying experience for both of us' (unlike *Cleopatra*), he nevertheless goes on to recount the immense strain that the role placed on Taylor:

It wasn't my screenplay; it was by Tennessee Williams and Gore Vidal. Their locutions were characteristically elaborate and stylized, not easy to commit to memory and demanding a great variety of approach in the playing. The last-act 'aria' of the girl, Catherine (Elizabeth), was as long and difficult a speech, I venture, as any ever attempted on the screen. It was also the dramatic climax of the film. There was no compromise possible: either it came off, or you could drop everything that had gone before into the out-take bin.

Well, after four or five takes I called a break; we'd been close, but no cigar. Maybe a short rest would do it. Then somebody, one of the gaffers I think, waved at me – and took me around behind the set. There, slumped on the floor beside a flat, was Elizabeth. Physically and emotionally exhausted. Sobbing in great dry gulps. Convinced she'd let herself and everybody else down. This was no 'showboat' for the benefit of agent, lover/husband, or just attention-getting; I'd seen too many of those, by masters of malingering, to be taken in. Elizabeth had quite simply been brought to her knees by her own demands upon herself. Her talent is primitive in its best meaning: she hadn't the techniques for rationing herself; her emotional commitment was total each time.

So I squatted beside her and made a very calculated suggestion, knowing damned well what the reaction would be. I proposed wrapping it for that day – and starting again, fresh, in the morning. I got the answer I expected. 'Tomorrow, my ass' (in effect), said Elizabeth, 'I'll do it now.'

She got up, fixed her make-up, Jack Hildyard hit the lights – and the next take was the print. Elizabeth's performance in *Suddenly, Last Summer*, particularly that last, long Williams 'aria,' was quite remarkable, I think. Run it again some time, and study it – objectively. If that's presently possible about anything Elizabeth does, or did.

Of course, it might not reflect the aesthetic implications of Antonioni's wall … but you'll rarely come across a more honestly realized performance by an actress.

(Mankiewicz interviewed by Carey [1972] in Dauth, 2008, pp. 113–14)

In suggesting how Taylor pushed herself to the limit during the filming of this harrowing final sequence, Mankiewicz highlights how, far from drawing on the kind of dispassionate studio-era techniques designed to reduce the emotional wear and tear on an actor, she was in fact displaying a total emotional commitment more redolent of Clift's acting ethos. In claiming, moreover, that 'you'll rarely come across a more honestly realized performance by an actress', he also presents an image of her as striving to achieve a dramatic conviction in her performance that mirrors the narrative's own search for truth. That Clift plays the role of the doctor seeking to extract from Taylor's character, Catherine, the truth of what happened the previous summer heightens the allegorical nature of this all the more. Indeed, on watching the sequence leading up to and including the flashback, it is possible to read this whole episode as a meditation on Taylor's collaboration with Clift and his capacity (as influential mentor figure) for drawing out a deeper emotional veracity in her acting.

During the sequence where he readies her for the dramatic disclosure that follows it is almost as if it is Clift the actor – not just the doctor – preparing Taylor behind the scenes for the big moment when she goes out to meet her audience as they wait for her in the garden of Sebastian's house. The self-reflexive nature of this scene is heightened by the fact that what Dr Cuckrowicz is trying to stimulate in Catherine is an exercise in memory recall – the very thing that was so central both to studio-era practitioners' and Strasberg's approach to acting. In the former case, this involved the creation of synthetic memory based on detailed study of the script, in the latter the substitution of personal memory for the character's own experiences. For both, however, the process served for the actor as an artificial means of preparation designed to facilitate access to a character's emotional life. Bearing this in mind, it is arguably the injection that Cuckrowicz gives Catherine in an attempt to trigger the release of her repressed trauma that more accurately comes to represent the artificial stimuli ordinarily used by actors to prepare themselves emotionally for a part.

Rather than simply endorsing such synthetic means for accessing someone's emotions, both Taylor and Clift's characters express scepticism about its efficacy during the initial part of this exchange. Thus, on being told by Cuckrowicz that the injection is 'Something different' from what she has had before, Catherine responds (with heavy sarcasm in Taylor's voice): 'The truth serum?' only for the doctor to reply: 'Yes, except there is no such thing.' 'As truth? Or the truth serum?' continues Catherine. 'There is truth all right' asserts Cuckrowicz: 'Somewhere.' Immediately, then, this encounter between them establishes a distinction between the reality of the character's experience (the 'truth' of what really happened last summer) and the illusion that there is some magical device for stimulating recollection of it. In rejecting the idea that there is such a thing as a truth serum, it is, moreover, as if Clift is asserting his own belief that there is some form of emotional reality that lies beyond this that Taylor as actor – not just character – must find.

The rest of this encounter reads very compellingly as a commentary on Clift's influence over Taylor and her sensitivity to this. Thus, having asked Catherine to 'close [her] eyes for a minute' and having shut the French door to the garden in an attempt to create a peaceful environment conducive to achieving the necessary introspection and focus, the doctor invites her to sit down. Then, on joining her in a nearby chair (having given her the injection), the following exchange ensues:

CUCKROWICZ Catherine – I want you to give me something.

CATHERINE Name it, it's yours.

CUCKROWICZ I want you to give me all your resistance.

CATHERINE Resistance? To what?

CUCKROWICZ To the truth.

CATHERINE Truth is the one thing I have never resisted.

CUCKROWICZ Sometimes people think they don't resist it, but they still do.

CATHERINE Sebastian said: 'Truth is at the bottom of a bottomless well.'

CUCKROWICZ Why did ...? Open your eyes. Why did you try to kill yourself?

CATHERINE Isn't that what everybody wants? Me out of the way? Mother and George would get their money. You'd get your building. Aunt Vi ...

CUCKROWICZ Go on.

CATHERINE You know what I think you're trying to do?

CUCKROWICZ What?

CATHERINE I think you're trying to hypnotize me. You're looking at me so ... straight. You're doing something strange to me with your eyes. Your eyes ... . Is that what you're trying to do?

CUCKROWICZ Is that what you feel I'm doing?

CATHERINE I feel ... peculiar. It, it doesn't just have to do with what you gave me.

CUCKROWICZ Catherine, I'm putting out my hands. I want you to put your hands into mine and give me all your resistance. Pass all the resistance from your hands into mine.

CATHERINE Here are my hands but there's no resistance in them.

CUCKROWICZ You'll tell the true story?

CATHERINE Yes, I'll try.

CUCKROWICZ Nothing not spoken. Everything told exactly?

CATHERINE Everything exactly. Because I have to.

This passage of dialogue is largely as Williams wrote it in his original play (bar a few minor modifications) but it gains immeasurably from Clift and Taylor's presence in the roles. In expressing Catherine's feeling that she is being hypnotised by the doctor, there is indeed a sense in which Taylor is voicing her own realisation of the powerful influence that Clift is exerting over her as an actor. The latter is not something, moreover, that can be explained simply in terms of a standard, externally imposed formula ('I feel ... peculiar. It, it doesn't just have to do with what you gave me') but, rather, according to a mesmerising quality that emanates organically from deep within his performing self: 'You're looking at me so ... straight. You're doing something strange to me

with your eyes. Your eyes … . Is that what you're trying to do?'
That she should highlight this particular feature as the source of
his creative power and influence seems especially apt given that the
eyes were regarded as the main conveyors of dramatic truth in film
acting. Indeed, in her study of acting techniques during the studio
era, Baron cites MGM drama coach Lillian Burns as saying that
for 'actors coming to film from theatre' they were required '[to
learn] projection from the *eyes* instead of just the voice' (1999,
p. 37).

Clift's understanding of this is summed up by biographer
Graham McCann: 'Throughout his career, he would often decide,
on set, to eliminate pages of dialogue, saying simply, "Just move in
close on my eyes"' (1991, p. 56). At the beginning of this book, we
explored how Taylor's awareness of the expressive possibilities of *her*
eyes manifested itself early in her career during *National Velvet*, so
that in Clift one could say that she found the perfect on-screen
collaborator to help her take this further. His recognition of the
intense on-screen bond that he and Taylor were capable of forging
through their eyes is suggested by the fact that in his working script
for *Suddenly, Last Summer*, 'Clift notes that at one moment
Cuckrowicz's and Catherine's "EYES LOCK" [written in caps]
and draws a padlock below' (Lawrence, 2010, p. 229). It seems
inconceivable that an actor so dedicated to his craft would not have
discussed his thoughts on this with the actress herself. Based on the
evidence of their actual performances, it seems almost certain that
they did, given how their dramatic interactions – from their first
meeting in the library of the psychiatric hospital – are punctuated
throughout by moments of this kind where their eyes lock together in
deep, intense stares. This focus on the eyes as the source of their on-
screen rapport is reinforced within the script itself. Thus, Catherine's
question: 'Haven't you noticed how oddly I've been looking at you?
… How I've been staring at your eyes?' is mirrored in her later
observation: '*You're doing something strange to me with your eyes.*'

'Where are you from?' asks Catherine
'Lions View' replies Dr Cuckrowicz

Such moments are crucial in forging the trust that develops between Taylor's character and Dr Cuckrowicz and, given the importance of this relationship to the film's narrative resolution, it's suggestive of how *Suddenly, Last Summer*'s preoccupation with discovering the truth that lies buried in the recesses of Catherine's repressed memory emerges out of the detail of these two actors' performances. The interplay between their eyes also destabilises the hierarchy inherent in their doctor/patient relationship, thereby initiating a process that is enacted in more extreme fashion through Taylor's vocal performance during the final flashback. Prior to that, her character is wont to express her reliance on Cuckrowicz at various points in the film. 'And you were the one who was going to help me. Help me. Help me!' Catherine cries in anguish on recovering from her ordeal with the male patients in the recreation area known as the Drum. During the scene where he asks her to pass all of her resistance over to him she asks him to order her to stand up, saying 'Tell me to. Then I think I could', only to then express her emotional vulnerability by asking him to allow her to kiss him: 'Hold me! I've been so lonely. Let me! Let me! Let me!' Yet, in acting terms, it is Taylor who gives the *tour de force* performance in the sequence that follows, Clift becoming increasingly marginalised as her character gradually moves from a state of dependency to autonomy, no longer in need of his narrative prompts (Cukrowicz/Clift: 'Go on.' Catherine/ Taylor: 'I am going on. Nothing could stop me now'). That this film was made three years after Clift's near-fatal car accident when he was in a much weakened state – struggling to cope both with the physical and psychological after-effects of that trauma and with the much greater demands that filming placed upon him as a result – adds another complexity to his role as facilitator rather than participant in this flashback sequence. According to McCann:

From the late 1950s onwards, Clift was obliged to husband his energy in a fairly ruthless way. It was too late in his career for him to alter his passionate, committed approach to performing, yet he no longer possessed the stamina to cope with long, demanding roles. He tried to concentrate on the cameo performance, the series of short scenes, the emotion-charged fragment. (1991, p. 71)

Bosworth also refers to how:

Throughout the filming of *Suddenly, Last Summer* Monty was consistently late on the set, and he had trouble remembering his lines. Katharine Hepburn became concerned. 'He used to have the most peculiar expression on his face. Whenever we'd shoot a scene, big beads of sweat would pop out on his forehead.' (Bosworth, 2007, [1978], p. 341)

Given Clift's impaired acting ability and his character's secondary narrative role during the flashback (as prompter of Catherine's memory), it is, then, as if he finds in Taylor an extension of his own performing self – someone through whom he can gain outlet for the emotionally intense and involved state of acting that he is so dedicated to but can no longer sustain himself due to his weakened health. This sense of them being two halves of a performing whole was in evidence right from the start of their collaboration in *A Place in the Sun*, when their striking physical resemblance – captured by director George Stevens in extreme close-up – made them appear as beautiful mirror images of each other. That film's famous close-up sequence of Taylor and Clift on the dance floor has been much discussed as the cinematic example *par excellence* of romantic union and the experience of falling in love (both at the level of one individual with another and the movie audience with their star idol) and the dissolution of boundaries that such a union entails (Lawrence, 2010, pp. 76–7). That Taylor and Clift were able to portray this collapsing of Self and Other can be partly explained in terms of their physical likeness and Stevens's much celebrated use of extreme close-ups to create this sense of their faces merging into each other. But it may also owe much to their shared commitment to total emotional involvement in character and losing oneself in the part.

Indeed, given Catherine's realization in *Suddenly, Last Summer* that Dr Cuckrowicz is doing something 'strange' to her with his eyes and considering Mankiewicz's account of the demands on Taylor during filming, it's possible to read her performance during the flashback as a fictional dramatisation, in the extreme, of this actor's influence over her as she, responding to his ethos of total emotional commitment, is driven (like her character) to the verge of collapse. But if Taylor's performance during this sequence can be understood as dramatising a moment in her career when, faced with Clift's mentoring presence on set, she almost succumbed to the dangers that she herself recognised in his passionate style of acting, then it's important to recognise the contributory role played by other factors. That *Suddenly, Last Summer* was Taylor's first venture into independent film-making following her initial break from MGM may well have created an added pressure for her to prove her worth as an actress. According to Mankiewicz, moreover, it was the extreme technical demands posed by Williams's lengthy last-act aria that placed such immense stress on her style of acting, the 'primitive' or instinctive nature of which was in certain respects quite different from Clift's more studied approach. As Taylor herself would recount in *England's Other Elizabeth*:

I think the first take is the most honest, the most spontaneous, you do things that just come to your head and nobody can stop you because you're filming. If they don't like it you do it again! But you get a sense of adventure. You get a rush, of like being that person, and what they would do. Not what *you* would do. What *they* would do. (2001)

In prioritising 'Not what *you* would do' but 'What *they* would do', Taylor defines her acting in ways that are consistent with the views of both studio-era practitioners and Clift himself, with whom she shared an intense dislike of Strasberg's technique of personal memory recall. Her emphasis on the spontaneity of the first take (and the 'rush' of 'adventure' this involves) is a far cry, however, from the studio-era 'practice of filling in characters' backgrounds' as 'part of the process of slowly and methodically entering into the world of the characters' (Baron, 1999, p. 40) not to mention Clift's own investment in extensive research and exhaustive rehearsals. For someone who favoured a more uncalculated approach, thriving on the spontaneity of the first take, the technical demands posed by filming the last-act aria in *Suddenly, Last Summer* must indeed have been trying and, in potentially detracting (in Taylor's eyes) from the honesty of her rendition by requiring multiple takes, they ironically militate against the very search for truth articulated by the film not just overtly in its narrative but implicitly at the level of performance. Taylor's well-noted ability to get into character quickly meant that, in less exceptional circumstances, she was usually able to commit her performance to film after a minimal number of takes, earning her the nickname 'One Take Liz'. Anthony Asquith summed up this facility of hers as follows:

Miss Taylor has the ability to get inside a part at a moment's notice. Once we had to start in the middle of a scene of great emotional intensity and it was as though the personal part of her were shed altogether and another part was assuming the character. She is astonishingly good at starting cold. She gets into the mood immediately when she steps in front of the cameras. And I have seldom known her to fluff a line.

Miss Taylor invariably rings true in her acting. Even when she makes a mistake, it's never because her emotion is forced or false. She may be aiming only at the wrong target. She is a 'natural' actress in the full sense of the word. She gives complete reality.

There is another thing. Like a fine musician, she thinks in relation to the complete score. She is aware of the other roles. Never, during the filming of 'The VIPs', did Miss Taylor intrude when a scene belonged to someone else.

On a film set, I try to create an atmosphere where actors are relaxed and tense at the same time – relaxed as people, but imaginatively stimulated as actors. It is my practice to say as little as possible. I like to say whatever I have to say beforehand. Whenever Miss Taylor walked onto the set, she knew exactly the point of the scene. I found the less said the better.

It can be dangerous, after an actor has done a scene well in rehearsal, to pick out points in the performance you thought were particularly good and ask him to duplicate it exactly in the take. What was fresh and spontaneous then may become forced and mechanical because the performer is subconsciously trying to reproduce the same effect.

People who have not worked with Miss Taylor may think of her only as a product of mass publicity, who has fascination because of her beauty. I must admit I was merely first prepared to meet and direct a beautiful girl whose talent was a carefully exploited thing. This was unjust. Miss Taylor is a serious actress. There is nothing frivolous about her work.

(Asquith, 1963, pp. 1, 7)

In his tribute to the actress, Paul Newman observed: 'She is not afraid to take chances in front of people. I was always staggered by her ferocity and how quickly she could tap into her emotions. It was a privilege to watch her' (2007). This facility for rapidly accessing a character's emotional state placed Taylor at odds with the practice of extensive rehearsal favoured by the Method school of acting (among others). She found a way of coping with this system by developing a strategy of holding back her emotions during rehearsals only to unleash them during the act of filming. As she recounts in *England's Other Elizabeth:*

In rehearsals I have *never* cried. Why waste it? And I get involved too and sometimes you just … don't play around with your own emotions that way. Your stomach gets upset and it's very hard sometimes to stop. So I wait … .

The minute the camera goes on something happens in me then I start to pull the stops. But when it's rehearsal my mind knows that this isn't the real thing. And some directors and actors, like, Paul Newman [he] evidently went up to Richard Brooks and said, 'Richard, I mean, is this it? Is this all she's gonna give?' And Richard said, 'It's OK, Paul, you wait.'

Although Taylor again concurs with the notion of herself as an instinctive actress without formal training or technique, this strategy of holding back emotionally is arguably a technique in its own right and one that seems in tune with other arts-related areas such as dance where performers often adopt the approach of initially running through or 'marking' their steps without dancing fully. This strategy of holding back emotionally in rehearsals can therefore be understood as a form of preparation developed by Taylor to suit her own more intuitive style of acting, one that differed fundamentally from the 'Method' by virtue of the fact that it was motivated by a desire to preserve/withhold rather than release/draw out the emotions required for the part. Given her concerns (quoted earlier) about the intense duress that Clift put himself through on set, it's an approach that also seems to have helped her cope more effectively with the demands that a commitment to total emotional involvement in character entailed. Indeed, returning to the point she made then that 'watching his intensity I learned not to let it kill you but that it wasn't … a game', one gets a sense from this of the actress striving to negotiate between the studio-era approach of 'dispassionate execution of performance' and the extreme method of acting on the edge that she found so compelling in her new co-star.

How she then managed to access her emotions so rapidly when it came to filming is another matter, of course, and, while not wishing to discount the idea that Taylor was a genuinely instinctive actress, I'd like to suggest that there is a way of thinking about this in more concrete terms. In so doing, I hope to demonstrate that Taylor drew on another approach, one that in certain respects seems similar to Clift's passionate style but that (predating her exposure to his working practices) might provide us with a key to understanding why she was able to achieve such intense involvement without the kind of exhaustive preparation and extensive rehearsal that he relied upon.

4 COMPASSION

In her memoir, Elizabeth Taylor recalls:

The first time I ever had to cry [on film] was in *National Velvet*. The horse was supposed to have colic, and of course he was Velvet's life. The scene was like a montage, covering the whole night – Velvet putting towels on him and hot water and rubbing him down, putting liniment on him. Finally, when the character Mickey played said he didn't think the horse would live, then Velvet cries.

I knew the scene and it hadn't worried me in the slightest because in those days I could summon up a few tears that would trickle down – but nothing like Margaret O'Brien. …

Anyway, we rehearsed the scene and Mickey put his arm around me and said, 'Honey, you know in this scene you have to cry.' And I said, 'Yes, Mickey, I know.' 'Well,' he said, you should think that your father is dying and your mother has to wash clothes for a living, and your little brother is out selling newspapers on the street and he doesn't have shoes and he's cold and shivering, and your little dog was run over.' It was like Chekov gone nuts and it was meant to make me start to cry.

Instead, I started to laugh, and I don't know what Mickey thought. Maybe he thought it was hysteria setting in. I didn't have the heart to say anything to him. I tried to control my giggles, but the more I tried, the more I couldn't stop them. When I did the scene, instead of imagining my father drunk and dying and my mother doing laundry in a snowy stream, all I thought about was the horse being very sick and that I was the little girl who

Velvet nurses her sick horse in *National Velvet* (1944)

owned him. And the tears came. But how generous of Mickey to try to help me. (Taylor, 1964, pp. 162–3)

In using this anecdote to illustrate her approach to acting,[1] it could be argued that Taylor does so in a way that once again conforms to the notion of herself as a naturally gifted actress who did not have to rely on formal technique. Yet what she is describing here is not some mystical, inscrutable outpouring of instinct but a way of relating to the situation through the recognisable emotion of compassion. So what exactly is meant by this term? According to the philosopher Nancy E. Snow:

Compassion is a 'suffering with' another that includes an altruistic concern for the other's good … . Compassion contrasts with pity. There is an immediacy or urgency about compassion that pity lacks. Perhaps this is best described by noting that pity is more spectator-like than compassion. We can pity someone while maintaining a safe emotional distance from what he or she is undergoing. When we feel compassion this emotional distance is crossed. We desire to relieve the other's plight, and in so doing, relieve ourselves of the burden of sharing the trauma caused by his or her condition. (1991, pp. 196–7)

If we relate this definition to the story of how Taylor was able to cry in *National Velvet*, then one could say that the actress's facility for producing the requisite tears owed much to her readiness to relinquish the 'safe emotional distance' that the studio-era practice of 'dispassionate execution of performance' required and adopt a position instead that involved a full sharing of the trauma caused by the suffering Other. Taylor's ability to accomplish this effect is all the more notable given that the compassion she is expressing is not just for her character but for the horse itself and, to understand her ability to connect so readily with this non-human realm of experience, it's helpful to refer to Erica Fudge's study of human–animal relationships in her book *Pets* (2008). Drawing on

Snow's work, Fudge stresses the importance of imagination as a way of achieving the identification necessary for compassion to exist: 'it is through "imaginative dwelling", through putting oneself "in the other's place", that compassion exists' (ibid., p. 66). Hence:

It is an imaginative leap in that I cannot prove that your pain and my pain are the same, but nor do I want to try to do that. My imaginative leap is, somehow, beyond proof and I respond to the suffering of another without the need for corroboration. (ibid., p. 67)

While acknowledging that 'Snow is not writing specifically about compassion for animals' (ibid., p. 66), Fudge suggests: 'It is possible to see how in her model compassion could be felt for a member of another species' and argues that pet ownership can be considered 'a form of "imaginative dwelling"' because 'the step from feeling for another human to feeling for another animal is not as great as it might appear to be' (ibid., p. 67):

Thus pet ownership, like compassion, requires imagination. To bring an animal into one's home, to live with it as a member of the family, is not simply to ignore difference; it is to engage in an ongoing process of translation. It is to make educated guesses that rely on both empirical observation ... and imagination. A thought that begins 'If I was a cat ...' could be relegated to the realm of 'mere' anthropomorphism, but it is also a productive – not to say compassionate – mode of cohabitation (ibid., p. 68).

Fudge contends that the act of reading fiction can be regarded, like pet ownership, as 'a model of compassion' (ibid.) since:

Many novelists ask their readers to care: to put themselves in the situation of the characters; to feel the horror or joy felt by a character. ... Fiction calls up compassion even as it takes us out of reality, and the two are not in opposition because compassion itself is an act of imaginative reading. (ibid., pp. 68–9)

Building on these two ideas, she proceeds to suggest that:

If pet ownership, like compassion, requires imagination, then clearly literature that focuses on pets might have something particularly important to say. Perhaps it is not just that novelists happen to be insightful about pets ... perhaps it is *because* they are novelists – are *imaginative* writers – that they are insightful. It might be that all of the problems that I have traced in this chapter are about reading. Thus, accessing an animal's inner life (what it is like to be an animal) is an act of the imagination. The attempt to have a conversation across the species barrier is not so different from the act of interpretation that is often involved in reading novels, which tell of lives not our own. Feeling compassion for and loving an animal is making an imaginative leap that is also like that required of us by many novelists. We connect with what is inaccessible by engaging ourselves in the process of understanding. (ibid., pp. 69–70)

It's interesting to note here that Taylor wrote *Nibbles and Me* (1946), a short book all about the escapades of her pet chipmunk, when she was just fourteen years' old. Her biographers have speculated on the extent to which MGM publicists saw this publishing venture (which began as a school essay) as a marketing opportunity to promote their new star in her follow-up film, *Courage of Lassie* (Mann, 2009, pp. 80–1). They have also pondered over its autobiographical significance, with Alexander Walker arguing that it unconsciously reveals the influence of Taylor's mother over her imagination (especially Sara's attitudes towards love and death and her affinity with late Victorian children's literature), not to mention the loneliness and emotional needs of the pubescent actress. He notes particular parallels between Taylor's book and Sara's favourite novel, Frances Hodgson Burnett's *The Secret Garden* (1990, pp. 51–5), drawing comparisons between the young actress's befriending of her chipmunk and the lonely Mary Lennox's attachment to the robin (a parallel that serves to reinforce the idea that Taylor's pet functions as a form of emotional compensation).

Brenda Maddox even reads it as prophetic of the actress's future relationships with men, referring to 'the chipmunk [as] a kind of Frog Prince, a lover in furry disguise' (1979 [1977], p. 53) and finding, in her reflections on how she was able to replace the original Nibbles on his death with a series of successors bearing the same name, a psychological rationale that may explain her later serial appetite for husbands (ibid., p. 55). Yet what tends to get lost in such accounts is the endearing sincerity of the book itself as a work of literature about pets and (bearing in mind Fudge's points) the highly developed capacity for imaginatively inhabiting the inner life of an animal that it reveals in the young author. The book begins with the line 'Ever since I was a little girl I have had all sorts of pets' and Taylor proceeds to relate how she developed a close bond of understanding with her first horse while still living in England at her family's summer retreat in the country:

I used to ride through the woods on my little mare Betty and I felt so high up in the air among the trees. It seemed as if I was right up there with the birds. They would fly down so low all around me and sing and chatter away – just as if they were trying to attract my attention and talk to me. I used to try and answer them, and sometimes Betty would whinny as if she wanted to talk to us too. She was so intelligent – she knew everything I said to her. Some people say horses do not understand what you say to them – that they only understand the tone of your voice in command – but that *isn't so*. I was only three and a half years old when I first had Betty, and she was as wild as anything, and threw me sky-high into a patch of stinging nettles the first time I crawled onto her back. Then I led her around and talked to her; I told her she had been given to me, and that I was her new mistress, and that I loved her very much and wanted her to love me. We walked around and talked for quite a while, and then I led her over to the stone wall where I could climb up and get on her back, and I kept on talking to her. From then on we were always friends. She would buck other people off or dash into the lake until she frightened them, so that they were glad to get off ... but you could do anything with her by talking to her. They said I was the only one who could do anything with her, but I know anyone could have if they had loved her as much as I did. (2002 [1946], pp. 1–2)

In a later chapter, she recounts her agonising decision to release Nibbles into the wild, observing how:

One day he sat there so long and so still, looking out of the window, my heart began aching for him … wondering what he was thinking … whether he would like to be out in the woods where he really belonged. (ibid., p. 63)

When it came to the moment where she was about to set him free, she recalls: 'I held Nibbles to my face and kissed and kissed him. I couldn't see – my eyes were so blinded with tears – but the feel of his dear little body I'll never forget' (ibid., p. 67). On watching him start off towards the woods, she says: 'My heart cried out to him, "Goodbye, Nibbles"' only to be thrilled to see him run back 'and jump[ed] up on my skirt and *into my hand,* where he gaily perched and finished his acorn'. 'Oh, I can't describe what I felt!' she exclaims, '*Then* there was no more doubt. He was *mine – by his own choice!* And he was as happy as I was – as we all were' (ibid., p. 68).

If Taylor's writing about her horse and chipmunk embodies that model of compassion identified by Fudge as a feature of broader literature about pets, then it's possible to understand her acting with animals in films in similar terms. Indeed, it may well have been this imaginative capacity that enabled her to make the kind of direct, intense connection with animals that comes through so forcibly in her performance in *National Velvet* and that might otherwise have been difficult to achieve without recourse to some form of simulated emotional response. Taylor's account of how Rooney got her to cry suggests that he was in fact offering her an informal variation on the kind of techniques later to become associated with the Strasberg school of Method acting. As we have already seen, this 'popularized the use of affective memory and the substitution of actors' personal experience for characters' circumstances and objectives' (Baron and Carnicke, 2008, p. 26), requiring actors to ask themselves: 'What in my own life would make me behave as the character?' (ibid.). It is a version of this substitution approach that Rooney appears to have offered Taylor, although in her case (presumably because of her youth), he asked her to draw not on actual experiences and memories but a fabricated, 'what if?' scenario of family misfortune. In so doing, he was, in effect, trying to elicit the other main response that Snow argues can induce a person to feel compassionate identification with a suffering Other – namely, 'the recognition of our own vulnerability', which, when achieved, convinces us of 'the belief that we are similar enough to others who endure misfortune to be susceptible to misfortune ourselves' (Snow, 1991, pp. 199–200).

Unlike Fudge, Snow makes an important distinction between this and 'imaginative dwelling' as the other main route to feeling compassion, arguing that: 'imaginative identification is not necessary for compassion' (ibid., p. 198). But she notes that, while effective, the 'recognition of our own vulnerability' to misfortune is not as creative a way of achieving identification and draws on Lawrence Blum's observation that: 'the talent for imaginatively dwelling on another's condition admits of degree, and … that not all compassionate persons have a well-developed talent' (ibid.). It is this alternative mode of response centred on 'a self-regarding concern with one's own weaknesses and consequent liability to misfortune' (ibid., p. 200) that Rooney seems to have been trying to elicit in Taylor. But the actress's anecdote suggests that her imaginative capacity was strong enough to render this alternative route to suffering compassion unnecessary: for her, the thought of the horse suffering was on its own enough to provoke tears, requiring no intermediary process of introspection or elaborate emotional fabrication (the incongruity of which instead prompts her uncontrollable laughter). Taylor's ability to respond directly to the horse's suffering thus suggests that her approach to acting was, like the on-screen child-star identity she projected on screen, much less bound by anthropocentric values than is traditionally the case since it didn't depend (as Rooney assumed) on her having to imagine some form of equivalent human scenario of suffering in her own life. Of course, the horse wasn't really ill – that too is a fabrication but, unlike the scenario Rooney constructs, her identification with the animal's suffering involves an act of imagination that is entirely consistent with the fictional reality of the story and the emotional life of the character she is playing.

It could be argued, then, that Taylor's approach to this scene involved a more direct and emotionally authentic form of acting than that proposed by Rooney and the Strasberg version of the Method to which his advice here seems closely allied. As such, it was also a form of acting that, because of its reliance on her imaginative capacity, was strongly centred around her own agency as a performer, the expression of which may have been aided by director Clarence Brown's tendency, apparently, to adopt a non-interventionist approach towards the actors on the set of *National Velvet* (Rooney, 1991, pp. 205–6). Contrast this with the approach adopted by Strasberg who, 'Despite [his] respect for acting … actually moved key elements of Stanislavsky's System from the actor's to the director's control, thus shifting artistic responsibility for performance' (Baron and Carnicke, 2008, p. 26). By encouraging substitution of 'personal feelings and emotions for that of the character', Strasberg's approach threatened to detach the actors from their characters and fellow actors while placing their own recalled emotions in the hands of the film-makers (ibid.). Taylor's account of how she responded to the demands of the scene in question suggests, by contrast, that her approach was instinctively more in tune with other less rigid forms of 'Method' acting than Strasberg's, bearing some affinity with Stanislavsky's interest in making an 'imaginative flight into the character's world' (ibid., p. 26) as well as Stella Adler's commitment to 'creative use of imagination' (ibid.).

The directness and immediacy involved in this compassionate form of acting helps explain, though, why Taylor was less drawn to the careful attention to script and exhaustive rehearsal practices considered so important by these non-Strasberg exponents of the Method as well as by studio-era practitioners and influential co-star Clift. Contemplating the role that compassion played in her work may therefore provide us with another way of thinking about her methodology as an actress, the imaginative properties of which have often been obscured by the more typical recourse to terms like instinct and intuition. Bearing in mind the earlier accounts given by her fellow actors and the directors she worked with, one might also reason more broadly that what has been termed as 'instinctive' acting on her part in fact involves a very real skill in being able to understand quickly what was required in emotional terms for a particular role, the talent for which may well owe much to her imaginative capacity for achieving compassionate identification with her characters.

One is faced with a possible irony here, in that the star who has received the most intense scrutiny of her private life and who the media has obsessed about so lengthily over the years, may actually be one of the least self-absorbed in her acting approach and someone who (despite the increasing pressure on her to act out fictional versions of herself and her off-screen dramas and romances) hated the Strasberg approach of drawing on personal experiences. This is not to rule out the possibility that Taylor at times drew on her experiences. Richard Brooks, who directed her on *Cat on a Hot Tin Roof*, has said that having to face the tragedy of her then husband Mike Todd's sudden death in a plane crash during the making of that film 'helped her grow up' and find a deeper emotional connection with the 'death and anguish' required in the script, although Taylor herself suggests that playing Maggie actually provided her with a vital escape from her own situation.[1] In his biography of Taylor, Spoto attributes her maturity of bearing as a child performer partly to the unnaturalness of her existence in the studio environment, constantly surrounded by adults (1995, p. 35), and the actress herself has written of her feelings of isolation and exclusion on growing up at MGM.

> Not being like other children, not belonging to the adult world and not belonging to a children's world, I felt always the outsider … . Horseback riding meant everything to me … . With kids my own age I was gawky and terrified. To them I was a freak. (1964, pp. 20–2)

Given all this, it's tempting to read Taylor's sensitive performance in *Jane Eyre* – as the kindly Helen compassionately reaching out to the friendless, ostracised heroine – as informed by the actress's own feelings of isolation and oppression as a victim of MGM's studio system. But these are aspects to Taylor's personality that appear to have emerged more strongly during her teenage years, as she began to resent the control exerted over her by the studio and her parents. It seems unlikely that such feelings were sufficiently developed to account for the kind of deeply realised compassion she displays either for the heroine in *Jane Eyre* or for the suffering dog and horse in *Lassie Come Home* and *National Velvet* respectively. Identification with the latter two would in any event be much more feasibly achieved, as discussed earlier, through an imaginative route (given their non-human status) and in *England's Other Elizabeth*, Taylor herself observes of that early phase: 'I had a great imagination and I just slid into it and it was like a piece of cake'.

Taking all this into account, it seems reasonable to surmise that Taylor already possessed this capacity for imaginative identification before any form of compassion based on recognition of her own vulnerability to suffering came into play. One might point, in turn, to her experience of working with animals during childhood as an important factor in facilitating this. In allowing her to explore and stretch her imaginative capacities in ways that went beyond the more typical human-to-human interactions, it provided an environment highly conducive to cultivating these creative tendencies in her as an actress. Of course, within these films Taylor had her own character to play (and, in the case of the horse-loving Velvet Brown, one whom she clearly related to very strongly). But in playing young girls who were themselves highly compassionate towards animals she was furnished with the perfect conduit for expressing this identification with the non-human Other. As such, these girl/animal narratives appear to have encouraged a creative fluidity between Taylor's performing identity and star persona. They created a scenario whereby compassion becomes both a potential method by which to achieve imaginative access to a character's world and the very emotion that (in playing a character identifying with the suffering Other) she has to realise within the performance itself.

This is not to suggest, of course, that this compassionate mode of response explains every aspect to Taylor's acting approach. As we explored earlier, several other influences should be taken into account and it may well be the case that, as her adult career progressed, this compassionate/imaginative approach developed in her childhood began to combine and merge with the passionate/ introspective style that she discovered in Clift. It's possible that Taylor may even have been exposed to another variation on Clift's passionate style of performance in childhood since her mother had been on the stage while an earlier popular and influential tradition of emotionalistic acting was still in evidence, albeit by then in decline (Wilson, 1966, p. 110).[2]

Contemplating the role that an imaginative form of compassionate identification played in Taylor's acting does supply a rationale, however, for understanding both her distinctiveness and vulnerability as a performer. Because if there was a character she was unable (for whatever reason) to feel compassion for (or imaginatively relate to in some other way), then she had none of the other standard techniques to fall back upon. To conceptualise Taylor's acting in this way may help explain, conversely, why, despite her professed loathing of a film like *Butterfield 8*, she was able to give such a fine performance in the role of Gloria Wandrous. Aside from basic professionalism, it may well have been that on some level she found a compassionate connection with her character and one thinks, especially here, of the scene where Gloria reveals her experience of sexual abuse as a child. It may also help to account for Taylor's intense on-screen rapport with Montgomery Clift, the two most successful films of the three they made together interestingly being those that afforded her greatest scope for expressing this emotion for his character. In *A Place in the Sun*, although still ostensibly typecast as the spoilt rich girl, during her scenes with Clift she moves far beyond the constraints of that kind of role, portraying Angela Vickers as a young woman who is not only supremely beautiful but endowed with a capacity for great tenderness and sensitive insight into the inner torment of George Eastman. This is established on their first meeting in the games room, when the actress walks around the billiard table towards Clift's character, asking at intervals: 'Why all alone? Being exclusive? Being dramatic? Being *blue*?' Through the elaborateness of this manoeuvre, Taylor finds scope to display that deep identification with the animal Other in her childhood films but which now, in this film marking her transition to adult stardom, she finds herself projecting onto the figure of the human outsider instead. Her ability to do so is facilitated by Stevens's use of two close-ups of her in the exchange that follows. That he doesn't offer an equivalent view of Clift during this initial conversation highlights the greater emotional access we are being granted to Taylor's character, but through this intimate view of her face it is as if she absorbs and reflects back at George something of his own unacknowledged sadness.

In *Suddenly, Last Summer*, Clift's more asexual role as doctor to Taylor's patient enables a now mutual sympathy to be expressed between their two characters. During their first encounter in the

library, she concludes her troubled, halting attempt to recount the night Catherine was raped at the Duelling Oaks by admitting, with lowered eyes: 'I'm trying to make you feel sorry for her', only to look up towards him by way of appeal: 'I hope I am.' 'I am sorry' says Cuckrowicz, staring back at her unflinchingly, the steadfast honesty in his eyes prompting her to declare (as she continues to return his intent look): 'I believe you really are.' Clift's role as doctor provides a rationale for such displays of understanding but what is striking is the extent to which Taylor's performance articulates an equivalent compassion in Catherine for him – despite the threat he poses her as a brain surgeon sent by her aunt to perform a lobotomy on her. From her very first sighting of Cuckrowicz, Catherine seems irresistibly drawn to some quality in him with which she feels a deep connection. Thus, following her accidental burning of the nun's hand with a lit cigarette during the library scene, she turns away in distraction. Pressing her hands against her head, she looks downwards in a gesture of despair, crying: 'Oh, I'm so sick of being bossed and bullied!', only to be brought out of this state of inner anguish by the doctor's appearance in front of her. Catherine reacts not with words but by fixing her eyes upon him in a wide-open, penetrating stare and, during his ensuing exchange with Sister Felicity (Joan Young), she continues this deep contemplation of his face, her brief glance back at the nun midway through only highlighting the contrasting profundity of the look she gives him as she turns back towards him. The more she gazes the more her initial bewilderment at his sudden appearance seems to transmute into fascination and then compassion as she becomes inexorably drawn to some inner mystery and sorrow residing within him. Cuckrowicz's position standing with his back to the camera focuses our attention on Catherine's reaction to him. So much so in fact that when she proceeds moments later to remark:

Besides, doctor, haven't you noticed how oddly I've been looking at you? … How I've been staring at your eyes: your beautiful, blue, frightened eyes. Why are they so frightened? Do you need help? Do you want help from me?'

we are left in no doubt as to the depth of sympathy he provokes in her.

Clift's own troubled state at this point in his career makes these expressions of compassion by Taylor's Catherine all the more poignantly apt and in registering this fear in his eyes, it is as if the actress responds to insecurities provoked in him by his 'ravaged postaccident face', the scars of which 'began to reveal the traces of a sorrow greater than that called for in his roles', making him 'incapable of creating a mask' (Hirsch, 1991, p. 175). In his account of Clift's role here, Hirsch goes on to observe that:

As the doctor in *Suddenly Last Summer* (1959), a part in which he has to investigate someone else's trauma while maintaining the pose of a disinterested scientist, he is cruelly miscast. He seems far more fragile than his patient, a terminally sane Elizabeth Taylor. (ibid.)

Yet it's the tension arising from this casting that contributes greatly to the film's complexity, providing a deeper rationale for Catherine's compassionate reaching out to his character. The disjuncture between Clift's role as capable neurosurgeon and his own troubled star identity also supports the play's own inherent interest in paralleling Dr Cuckrowicz (supposed figure of normality and reason) with Catherine's dead gay cousin (a link also alluded to by comments about the likeness of their eyes). This destabilisation of the film's normative strategies is heightened all the more by Taylor's role in the flashback, when she literally becomes the voice of Sebastian.

In *The Celluloid Closet: Homosexuality in the Movies*, Vito Russo compares the film's portrayal of Sebastian with the treatment of the monster in the horror film, arguing that the concluding scene where

the creature is finally destroyed by an angry mob of street urchins in a climax [is] not much different from that of James Whale's *Frankenstein*, in which the peasants pursue the monster to the top of a hill, where fire engulfs him. (1987, p. 116)

Yet in focusing only on the visual and narrative aspects to this sequence, Russo overlooks the important affective role that Taylor's voice plays throughout. It is not just that she actually speaks Sebastian's words at certain points in her narration and, in fact, on those occasions when she does, her voice develops a harsher, biting quality that tends to reinforce the more negative image of her cousin as a controlling figure. Rather, it is her vocal performance during Catherine's own account of what happened that is so powerful, enacting as it does not only *her* trauma as she begins to recover her memory of what happened, but that endured by Sebastian himself during the moments leading up to his death. At one point midway through the flashback, for example, when recounting his departure from the restaurant, she conveys a sense of his mounting panic and terror through her dramatic delivery of the line: 'He *fled* from the place.' She emits the word 'fled' with a sudden increase in pitch and intensity, the explosion of feeling it creates making the sound balloon suddenly outwards, erupting out of the sentence in a way that vividly enacts both the drama of the action itself and the fear welling up inside Sebastian that he cannot admit to.

Then, as her narration reaches its climax, she employs an extreme version of the hyperventilating style of delivery she had used earlier when expressing her character's anxiety at the prospect of the lobotomy. On this occasion, the increasingly slow, spasmodic nature of her delivery powerfully evokes Catherine's troubled state even more complexly than before – as narrator, in the present tense struggling to confront the most horrifying part of her repressed memory, and as participant within the flashback, as she chases after her cousin. At the same time, it acts out the traumatic experience of Sebastian himself, his acute palpitations and fatigue on running up the hill in a desperate attempt to escape the pursuing mob coming through most forcibly in the gasping rhythms of her voice. It's a form of vocal performance that is strongly reminiscent of that moment in *National Velvet* when Velvet stands up to her father's pressure to take up the offers for her and The Pie to go to Hollywood by recounting what the horse did for her in the Grand National. On that occasion, her ability to convey Snow's notion of compassion as 'a "suffering with" another' (1991, p. 196) is evident in the way that she identifies with the extremity of the horse's effort through her performance. Pushing her delivery to breaking point, she cries out: 'He b*uuurr*st his heart for me!' and reenacts through the rising pitch and accelerated patterns of her voice the increasing demands placed on the animal's body as he is pressed to go ever faster over the fence-strewn course. The intensity of Taylor's performance also endows Velvet's emotional relating to the horse with an 'immediacy' and 'urgency' that make it powerfully expressive of compassion rather than pity. Refusing the spectator-like position associated with the latter, Taylor's reenactment of the horse's act of 'bursting' his heart for her ensures that any such 'safe emotional distance' is crossed.

In both films, Taylor identifies with the suffering of another by pushing her voice to the emotional limit, manipulating its rhythm, pitch and timbre in ways that reenact the experience of the person/animal she describes (note the specific parallels, for example, between her explosive delivery of the words 'burst' and 'fled'). The contexts within which such performances take place seem very different but the underlying similarities between them highlight how this compassionate mode of acting, which originated during her childhood years, feeds into her adult work and in a way that once again articulates a strong imaginative identification with the Other in society. Another example of this can be found, more controversially, in the Holocaust documentary *Genocide* (1982) where Taylor narrates, in voiceover, the personal testimonies of Jewish people who witnessed the atrocities committed by the Nazis firsthand. The two most notable sequences consist of those where she recounts first Rivka Yosselevska's horror on seeing her family members murdered before being shot at herself and falling alive into a pit of dead and dying bodies, and then the experience of a young boy, Leon Kahn, as he watches in terror from behind a cemetery wall as the Nazi soldiers rape, mutilate and murder their victims in cold blood. In performing this role, Taylor (who had herself converted to Judaism in 1959) reprises an on-screen association with Jewishness that had begun thirty years before with her role as Rebecca in *Ivanhoe*. In casting the actress in that earlier part, MGM unwittingly acknowledged a transgressive quality to Taylor's own beauty, associating it with a threatening Otherness that has to be contained.

In *Suddenly, Last Summer*, her ability to identify with Sebastian's suffering through the non-linguistic dimensions of voice challenges the restrictions imposed by censorship, conveying a sensitivity to the inner emotional life of a character otherwise denied a subjectivity of his own. The collapsing of the boundary between Self and Other that Taylor's performance enacts has been construed pessimistically by certain queer readings, however, as entailing a loss of identity for her character. According to D. A. Miller's account, for example, Catherine is reduced to the role of a mere stand-in for Sebastian, acting as a device or conduit for the telling of his story. The loss of subjectivity this involves is seen as reflected in the gradual elimination of her body from the frame. As Lawrence states (summarising this aspect to Miller's reading): 'Reduced to a mere voice, like Echo, the woman is "without substance"' (Lawrence, 2010, p. 226). It's important to bear in mind, though, that, in recalling what happened last summer, Taylor's character is also confronting the anguish of her own rape trauma and it's precisely this that can be understood to underpin her identification with Sebastian's situation. In narrating Catherine's story, Taylor is also (in a triumphant overcoming of the technical difficulties that Mankiewicz says she experienced on set) expressing something fundamental about her own identity as an actress, the virtuosity of her performance in that dramatic climax leading this author to concur with Richard Dyer's view that there is nothing 'mere' about her voice.

One only has to consider how some of Taylor's finest performances often rest (as in this case) upon extended monologues for proof of how crucial her voice is to the expression of her star identity although, as her hilarious performance on the American CBS television show *What's My Line?* (1954) demonstrates, it is much more chameleon in nature than those belonging to stars like Bette Davis and James Stewart. In Taylor's episode, she manages to baffle the blindfolded judges for some considerable time by adopting a high-pitched, squeaky Southern drawl. In their equivalent slots, by contrast, Davis and Stewart find it impossible to disguise their distinctive vocal patterns and colouring, so much so that they are found out almost immediately (the situation, in Davis's case, is exacerbated by the fact that she had laryngitis at the time). That Stewart and Davis were unable to alter their voices could be regarded as proof of a stronger, more unshakeable star identity, one wherein the voice resists being de-anchored from the actor's body. Yet Taylor's ability to manipulate her voice is exactly what makes it such a flexible and highly appropriate instrument for achieving total involvement in character: that desire to become the person one plays. Such elasticity may help explain why Dyer reads Taylor's voice as expressing a certain indeterminacy of desire although rather than being one that 'wants something else, her own pleasure', in films like *Suddenly, Last Summer* its expressive force derives, conversely, from its facility for expressing an intense imaginative identification with the Other's pain.

CODA: MOVING ON

It's dawn and George (Richard Burton) and Martha's (Elizabeth Taylor) guests have just departed. The rage and bitter recriminations that went before have subsided and the couple are left contemplating the void suddenly created by his killing off of their imaginary child. Switching off the last remaining light in the room, George observes with a slow, aching melancholy: 'Sunday tomorrow. All day' then walks over towards Martha by the window. Alex North's opening nocturne meantime resumes softly on the soundtrack, the initial slow pulse of a harp amid melodic guitar signalling a returning heartbeat in their relationship. Standing beside his wife, George places his left hand supportively on her shoulder while Martha, her face still wrestling with grief, continues to sit looking straight ahead. The harsh contrapuntal style of their earlier warring dialogue is replaced here by a much gentler, more fluid pattern of alternating enquiry as Taylor's character grapples with the reality of their situation. 'Did you ... Did you have to?' she asks haltingly. 'Yes', says George tenderly. 'It was ... You had to?' she appeals once more, searching for reassurance. 'It was time' he replies.

Twenty-two years after Taylor's star-defining role in *National Velvet*, the actress finds herself seated once more by the window, confronting some major loss, and being consoled, in the film's closing sequence, by a figure intent on convincing her of the need to move on. Back then, Mrs Brown sought to help her daughter come to terms with the sudden departure of her friend Mi by reinvoking the speech she had made in the attic, maintaining that Velvet had already proven by her rejection of the chance to go to Hollywood that she 'knew that the race was over and *it was time* to go on to the next thing'. The shooting of the horse in *Giant* dramatises another key moment of loss and, interestingly, that scenario once again finds the actress positioned by the window (this time standing facing it rather than sitting with her back to it) and now comforted by Rock Hudson's character who, like Burton, has to kill off the object of her affection. In that case, Leslie's loss is compensated by the survival of the sick Mexican baby but in *Who's Afraid of Virginia Woolf?*, it is the killing of the couple's own illusory child that Taylor's character must confront. Hudson's assertion that '*Somebody had to do it*' thus finds its more contested reworking in Martha's anguished cry (on first taking refuge by the window): 'You didn't have to kill him! ... You didn't have to have him die. ... That wasn't needed' then (with George now beside her), 'Did you have to do it?' while Jordan's follow-up comment – 'I thought *it'd be better* if it was me' – obtains a more distant echo in George's assurance to Martha that '*It will be better* ...'.

Viewed together, these moments reveal the continuities as well as developments in Taylor's career as a movie actress, most noticeably highlighting a capacity for subtle restraint that has often been overlooked by this star's association with excess. In *Giant*, this quality is partly compounded, partly obscured by the director's detached camerawork but in *National Velvet* and *Virginia Woolf*, the effect is fully concentrated in the actress's own performance. Sitting almost motionless and staring straight ahead for much of the time, her eyes cast sorrowfully downwards, she conveys through this extreme holding in of her performing self her characters' difficulty in moving on, presenting them as caught in liminal moments of crisis and reflection. It is only through her understated interactions with the person next to her that she hints at a tentative reemergence

from this position of stasis. This is expressed in *National Velvet* through Velvet's slow shaking of her head in response to her mother's question as to whether she would want to deprive Mi of his chance 'to leave … and make his way in the world', the heavy weighting she attributes to this movement suggesting a maturity of understanding just starting to assert itself amid feelings of resistance and loss. In *Virginia Woolf*, the effect is more complex, since Martha's short bursts of vocal and physical energy occur at points when she tries to contest George's decision and persuade him of the need to reclaim their world of illusion, her movement towards acceptance of her situation and the uncertainty of their future together finding expression in a more muted, hesitant form of delivery.

Inclining her head slightly towards George at one point, she asks with rising panic in her voice, 'Just us?' 'Yes' he replies softly. Turning further towards him, she appeals: 'You don't suppose maybe we …?', 'No' he says, breaking in firmly. 'Yes!' she insists urgently only to follow this with a despondent 'No' of her own, looking resignedly away from him again, her head now more lowered. 'All right?' enquires George tenderly after a while. 'Yes' says Martha quickly then, pausing and looking further away to her left, she counters this with an even more despairing 'No', closing her eyes momentarily. Staring intently at her as before, George begins to sing the refrain she had made up at the party and which had earlier provoked such raucous laughter in her. 'Who's afraid of Virginia Woolf? Virginia Woolf, Virginia Woolf?' he chants quietly. A wave of palpable fear rushes across Martha's face as she looks upwards and, instinctively reaching across to grasp his hand, she closes her eyes and whispers: 'I am, George.' 'Who's afraid of Virginia Woolf?' he continues. 'I am George. I am' she reiterates in hushed tones. Having opened her eyes just prior to this last refrain of his, she closes them once more on uttering her final 'I am', slowly bowing her head as the camera, advancing towards her, brushes past her face, moving in on the image of their hands clasped together in mutual need and support.

Taylor's realisation of Martha's despair in the film's closing sequence is much more nuanced and sustained than her rendering of Velvet's devastation at Mi's departure and, in contrast to the equal interplay between her and Hudson during their equivalent moment by the window in *Giant*, here she is the undoubted focus of our attention, Burton himself showing commendable discipline in acceding to the priority of her performance. The intimacy the camera establishes with her face is also much more intense and uncompromising than that parallel moment in *National Velvet*, her yielding to the full force of its scrutiny in the last few seconds mirroring Martha's final facing up to her deepest fears and insecurities. Yet, these are differences of gradation rather than approach and, in managing to reach beyond this woman's harsh exterior and find the vulnerable being that lies beneath, Taylor displays a compassion for her character that seems once more deeply rooted in her work as a child actress. In her memoir, she offers an interesting account of how she imagined Martha, using an analogy that is particularly suggestive of the important role that animals played in cultivating this compassionate identification with character (the italics in the following quote are mine):

I wanted to create my own Martha who had nothing to do with anybody else's Martha. I think she is *a desperate woman who has the softness of the underbelly of a baby turtle. She covers it up with the toughness of the shell*, which she paints red. Her veneer is bawdy; it's sloppy, it's slouchy, it's snarly. But there are moments when the façade cracks and you see the vulnerability, the infinite pain of this woman inside whom, years ago, life almost died but is still flickering. (Taylor, 1964, p. 156)

In *Boom!* (1968), Taylor would face the challenge of playing another complex woman – the terminally ill Flora 'Sissy' Goforth –

whose loud, caustic exterior serves in that case as a denial of her own impending mortality. Refusing to accept the fact that she is dying for much of the film, gradually – through the influence of Burton's character, Christopher Flanders, who visits her in his role as 'Angel of Death' – she admits to the reality of her situation. Even then, however, she remains defiant. Rejecting his warning 'That tough as you are, you are not so tough that one day perhaps soon you're going to need someone or something that'll mean God to you. If it's only a human hand or a human voice,' she insists that she doesn't want to be escorted 'to the eternal threshold' but 'want[s] to go forth alone'. With her physical condition rapidly deteriorating, though, she is forced to request that he assist her back to her room and, once there, asks him not to leave her alone, allowing him to narrate a story of how he discovered his vocation in life as she lies dying in bed. As in *Virginia Woolf*, it is Burton's character once more by her side as she lies near the open window, the white lace curtains wafting in the ocean breeze as the life ebbs away from her. Following her death, a brief interlude ensues showing Flanders now out on the veranda, dropping the ring he had earlier removed from Sissy's finger into a wine glass then throwing both away onto the rocks below. We are then presented with a shot of her corpse lying on the bed and, as the film slowly dissolves from this to one of the ocean waves crashing beneath, Flanders can be heard uttering his familiar awakening call of 'Boom!' for the last time. It's a stunning end to a film often regarded as marking the beginning of a decline in Taylor's movie-star career, the moment where Sissy 'goes forth' being realised, through this superimposition of the actress's body over the shot of the ocean, in a way that accords this star a now more final, elemental merging with nature. If this makes *Boom!* seem more deeply in tune with the spiritual values of Zen Buddhism that Tennessee Williams was exploring at the time of writing the play[1] on which the film is based (Paller, 2002), then it also completes that pattern of transition and moving on that runs complexly (and with various forms of resistance)

The deathbed scene in *Boom!* (1968)

throughout Taylor's career, offering elegiac testament to her capacity to articulate the notion of the individual's journey through life.

During the course of my writing this book, Elizabeth Taylor herself passed away, sadly, on 23 March 2011. If the greatness of a star can be measured, above all, by the sense of cultural loss her death generates then, in her case, the extraordinary global response to such news is proof of her lasting, multifaceted impact. At the time of her death, many paid tribute to her wider contribution to the cause of humanity: 'We have just lost a Hollywood giant. More importantly, we have lost an incredible human being,' said Elton John while Barbra Streisand concluded: 'She made her life count.' Actor Martin Landau (who appeared with Taylor in *Cleopatra*) described her as 'a unique talent and a singularly spectacular individual' while the actress's oldest son, Michael Wilding Jr, wrote:

Though her loss is devastating to those of us who held her so close and so dear, we will always be inspired by her enduring contribution to our world. Her remarkable body of work in film, her ongoing success as a businesswoman, and her brave and relentless advocacy in the fight against HIV/AIDS, all make us all incredibly proud of what she accomplished. We know, quite simply, that the world is a better place for Mom having lived in it.[2]

In her later years, Taylor herself came to regard her humanitarian work in fighting to eradicate AIDS as her most important legacy and it would be hard to disagree with that. But her death has also thrown into sharper relief than ever the importance of reassessing her achievements as an actress.

An actress who managed, among other things, to make an art out of compassion.

NOTES

Introduction

1 According to Allen Estrin, it was Brown's collaboration with ingénue
   performers like Taylor in the 1940s that enabled him to rediscover the
   very vitality to his film-making that he had shown in his earlier silent work
   with the young Garbo and other 'neophyte film actors who under his
   guidance developed into major stars' (Estrin, 1980, p. 144). Attributing a
   decline in the quality of Brown's films during the 1930s to his increasing
   work with established stars whose 'films were primarily showcases for
   their screen personas', he suggests:

   > Perhaps we ought to view Brown's shift after 1935 to films involving young actors in
   > the lead roles as an effort to regain his artistic integrity: when directing young actors
   > like Elizabeth Taylor or Claude Jarman, he was working with 'raw material' which he
   > could fashion to fit his needs. He had no responsibilities to the young actors' screen
   > personas other than what he himself dictated. And so it is indeed the case that
   > Brown's best sound films – *Ah, Wilderness, National Velvet, The Yearling* and *Intruder
   > in the Dust* – all involve young heroes played by actors who had little or no screen
   > experience. (ibid.)

2 In a *Mirror News* article entitled "Liz Is a Whiz as a Grandmother',
   entertainment editor Dick Williams speculates on Taylor's next role after
   the one in *Giant*: 'If it's "Raintree County," Elizabeth is hoping to play the

bad girl' he observes before quoting her as saying: 'I'm so tired of playing poised, sweet rich girls' (Williams, 1955). In 'The Elizabeth Taylor Story', an article published in three parts in *Look Magazine*, Eleanor Harris highlights the star's lack of egotism about her career but goes on to cite her desire to better herself professionally:

> When the subject of acting is brought up, she replies, with a deprecatory laugh, 'Don't ask *me* about acting.' Then she adds, 'But some day, I think I will be an actress. I'm now learning and developing; I'm trying. … The reason I suddenly became interested in acting in the past two years is that I finally got tired of all the garbage,' she says. 'In 15 years, I've only made four pictures I really loved: *National Velvet*, *A Place in the Sun*, *The Last Time I Saw Paris* and *Giant*. I also love the picture I'm making now, *Raintree County*. But how would you like to act year after year in movies with no story content? I've made up my mind that I'll only do films I'm enthusiastic about. I've been good so few times – but I would like to be good.' (Harris, 1956, pp. 120–1)

3   Others have commented more favourably on Taylor's stage work, particularly her role as Regina in *The Little Foxes*. William J. Mann, for example, claims of her debut Broadway performance in that play on 7 May 1981 that: 'She didn't miss a beat that night. Her voice was strong and full. Her magnificent eyes seemed to reach the farthest seat in the theater' (2009, p. 403). He cites Dennis Christopher, the actor cast as her nephew, as saying: 'She had such a power about her that night … By the time we opened on Broadway – and I'm really a theater snob, so I don't say this lightly – she was brilliant, indelible, on fire' (ibid.: 404). Such stage success is at times attributed more to personality than acting talent, however. Thus, both Mann and Alexander Walker quote from the *New York Times*'s review of the play's opening night. '[Regina's role] doesn't require great acting,' Frank Rich said; then, placing his finger on the dramatic pulse of the evening, he added, 'but it does require the tidal force of pure personality' (Walker, 1990, p. 349). Mann nonetheless refers to Taylor's 'new – and in some ways feminist – interpretation of Regina'

(2009, p. 400) as 'very different from those played by Tallulah Bankhead and Bette Davis' (ibid., p. 404).

4   Taylor was nominated five times in the 'Best Actress' Oscars category for her performances in *Raintree County*, *Cat on a Hot Tin Roof* (1958), *Suddenly, Last Summer* (1959), *Butterfield 8* (1960) and *Who's Afraid of Virginia Woolf?*, the last two films being the ones for which she won the awards.

1 Riding to stardom

1   In Bagnold's novel, Rooney's character Mi is already an established member of the Brown family at the start of the story and there is a reference later to him having a girlfriend (2000 [1935], pp. 110–11).

2   In her reading of the film, Gaylyn Studlar acknowledges that the film does 'capture something of her [Velvet's] rapturous feelings for the horse' during 'later scenes of her riding the Pie in long shot'. She also notes that while 'there is no physical sexual relationship suggested between Velvet and Mi … the film does suggest an emotional sympathy between them that has romantic potential', adding 'the casting of the diminutive Rooney lends a kind of physical symmetry between the two (they are almost the same height) that adds to the viewer's perception that they are destined to be a couple' (2010, p. 31). She doesn't refer, however, to the significance of narratively juxtaposing Velvet's first encounter with Mi with the one with The Pie nor indeed the parallels suggested by their rhyming names. Overall, she argues that any sexual undercurrents to Velvet's relationship with her horse are successfully negotiated and contained, maintaining: 'So that Velvet's intense feeling for horses remains a buoyant, uplifting emotion rather than a low sexual one, the film works to de-eroticise Taylor at key moments' (ibid., p. 30).

3   In Bagnold's novel, Velvet names the horse The Pie as an abbreviation of the word 'piebald' and this occurs relatively late on in the story after they have entered him for the Grand National (2000 [1935], p. 144). That the

screenwriters decided to retain the same name even though the horse that played this role in the film is not a piebald suggests their awareness of the potential in this link with Rooney's character. 'Pirate' actually abbreviates more logically to 'Pi' rather than 'Pie' and, interestingly, while the latter was retained in the script, MGM's Program Notes (1944c) and other production material refer to the horse as 'The Pi', a name that suggests greater symmetry with Mi. Given Mi's own wayward inclinations (he is later shown being tempted to steal first the Brown family's savings and then the 100 gold sovereigns he is charged with taking to London as entry money for the Grand National), Ede's branding of the horse as a 'Pirate' reinforces this link even more. One might also enlist in support of this parallel Mi's later description of himself when expressing resentment at his sense of class exploitation: 'What's a horse? An animal that earns his keep by breaking his back. I'm a horse, and I'll be one till I use my head again.'

4   Alexander Walker argues that during the actress's early teen years, 'Animals took the place of boys in Elizabeth's interests outside her family' (1990, p. 51), while Brenda Maddox reads her affection for chipmunks as prophetic of the actress's future relationships with men (1979 [1977], pp. 53–5). For further discussion of the latter, see Chapter 4 of this book.

5   In *Animal*, Erica Fudge cites Freud's observation that: 'Children show no trace of the arrogance which urges adult civilised men to draw a hard-and-fast line between their own nature and that of all other animals' and she goes on to argue that: 'The question of the child's lack of arrogance that Freud finds is certainly central to many of the classic children's books of the last century' (2002, p. 70). In *Picturing the Beast: Animals, Identity, and Representation*, Steve Baker discusses how children's close rapport with animals has been understood in terms of their animistic way of thinking about the world. Animism refers to the belief that (in Bruno Bettelheim's words): 'there is no clear line separating objects from living things; and whatever has life has life very much like our own' and that 'because of this inherent sameness it is believable that man can change into animal, or the other way around' (Bettelheim quoted in Baker, 2001 [1993], p. 123).

6   For another example, consider the much later scene in the horse trailer the night before the race at Aintree when Velvet asks Mi to cut her hair. Having searched in the trunk for the implements needed to carry this out, Velvet sits down on a barrel and says with a gentle whinny of a laugh: 'The Pie won't mind you using his scissors on my mane.'

7   Referring to this 'dazzling close-up' of Taylor, Liz Burke also notes that the actress 'is as passionate as Joan of Arc when she states: 'I'd sooner have that horse happy than go to heaven' and admits to this being 'One of [her] favourite lines in cinema' (2002).

8   The 'Velvet Girl' article also tells of the time when Taylor, still a young child back in England, enthusiastically befriended a chimpanzee during a visit to London Zoo: there, her Darwinian-like delight at being embraced by the chimpanzee as if she were one of his own is implicitly contrasted with the guards' approach of using aggression in the form of the butt of a gun to control the animal (Arnold, 1945, p. 90).

9   'The child puts a spell on birds and beasts and studio bigwigs. With birds and beasts she holds familiar conversation, like the troubadour saint of Assisi, and they follow her about performing as she pleases' (Howe, 1945, p. 99). St Francis of Assisi preached the unconventional Christian view that animals are man's brothers and sisters and that it is the responsibility of humans to act as stewards of the natural world rather than exert dominion over it.

10 It's worth noting that Enid Bagnold herself was not only a keen horsewoman but also served as an army nurse during World War I (Bagnold, 2009 [1918]). The sequence in the stable where a frightened Velvet reveals to Mi that her father (a butcher by trade) has threatened to 'send The Pie to the knacker's yard for cat's meat' (following his destruction of the family cart) acquires a deeper resonance within this wartime context. The grand ambitions that she reveals directly afterwards for the horse are motivated precisely by a desire to show that 'With half a chance he'll prove he belongs in the history books and not in the knacker's yard.' Elsewhere, the film's pastoral tone means that it doesn't dwell on the grimmer realities of animal oppression as strongly as Bagnold's novel,

which persistently portrays Mr Brown's slaughterhouse as located right next door to the family's sitting room (2000 [1935], p. 2).

2 The animal returns

1   *National Velvet* was, in fact, filmed not in England but at Pebble Beach, California although, for the purposes of describing the story's fictional world, it is referred to here as the Sussex Downs.

2   Taylor's association with the horse first reemerges in her adult career in *The Girl Who Had Everything* (1953), a moralistic remake of the Norma Shearer star vehicle *A Free Soul* (1931). There, she plays an impetuous, strong-willed young woman, Jean Latimer, who has been brought up by her single-parent attorney father, Steve (William Powell), to think for herself (that is, in traditional terms, like a man). She comes into conflict with him, however, when she turns down his preferred conventional male suitor, Vance (Gig Young), in favour of the charismatic but dangerous Victor Ramondi (Fernando Lamas), leader of a gambling mafia outfit and former client of her father. While much less accomplished than *Giant*, *The Girl Who Had Everything* is notable for being the first film in the actress's adult career that allows her to play this kind of independent-minded female and, significantly, this is accompanied by a nascent resurfacing of various forms of equine imagery (including an episode where Ramondi, outbidding Vance, buys a colt at an auction and gives it to Jean only for her to be ordered to return it by her father).

3   It's also worth noting that early in his own career at the Hal Roach Studios, Stevens acted as assistant cameraman on three silent films that featured 'a beautiful black stallion named Rex The Wonder Horse' (*Black Cyclone* in 1925, *The Devil Horse* in 1926 and *No Man's Law* in 1927, all directed by Fred Jackman) (Moss, 2004, pp. 15–17). This experience may be another factor that helps account for the unusual sensitivity that Stevens displays towards the horse's point of view in *Giant*.

4 In going on to stress Velvet's staunch protection of the horse, *National Velvet* eschews the convention of darker child/animal narratives where the killing of the beloved animal companion marks a rupture in the child's idyllic rapport with nature, signalling a need to come to terms with the realities of growing up.

5 For another example of this, consider the moment in *The Sandpiper* where an enraged Taylor fights off Ward Hendricks's (Robert Webber) aggressive sexual advances. Responding to his threat that: 'If I wanted you right now, there is nothing that you could say or do about it' and his attempt to pull off her clothes, she turns on him like a cornered animal and, picking up an axe, screams: 'You do it, and I'll kill you!'

6 In a *Photoplay* piece entitled 'Vaguely Wonderful' by Faith Service, Michael Wilding is quoted as saying that:

> Life with Liz is never shared with less than five pets ... [she] loves to adopt them, especially if they're scrawny, and build them back to health. ... I would hate to go on an African safari with Liz. She would literally Bring Them Back Alive – and turn the house into an informal zoo. (1955, p. 77)

A *Photoplay* article by Herb Lowe entitled 'Liz Takes French Leave' follows a similar line, describing the Wilding house in Beverly Hills as 'an animal shelter' wherein the non-human inhabitants enjoy a life of movie-star luxury (Lowe, 1954, p. 115). In 'Vaguely Wonderful', Wilding is also reported as saying that they have a duck that: 'lives on Elizabeth's shoulder', remarking 'When she leaves the room without him, he shrieks. The duck, when young, was put in the baby's play-pen. He has now outgrown this and is given the run of the house' (1955, p. 77). Another duck appears in Edward Murrow's *Person to Person* television interview with Taylor and Mike Todd (1957), when the actress is shown cuddling the young animal as it nestles into her as she sits on the couch with her then third husband, even becoming the subject of discussion at one point. In *Furious Love*, Sam Kashner and Nancy Schoenberger claim that the Burtons' meeting with director Franco Zeffirelli to discuss the possible casting of them in *The Taming of the Shrew* was disrupted by the antics of Taylor's latest pet, 'a tiny, leaping African primate known as a "bush baby"', and that it was only the director's willingness to help the actress in retrieving this animal that persuaded her to play Kate (2010, pp. 165–6). Alexander Walker maintains that Taylor's separation from Senator John Warner was precipitated by her refusal to move into an apartment that 'had a firm rule against keeping pets'. 'She wouldn't be separated from her pets', concludes Walker, 'She chose instead to be separated from her husband' (1990, p. 350).

7   Rather tellingly, the decline of Taylor's movie-star career from the late 1960s onwards is marked by a noticeable tailing off of her on-screen rapport with animals and nature and, although it resurfaces later in *The Blue Bird* (1976) and the made-for-television film *There Must Be a Pony* (1986), never again would it be realised with the same intensity or conviction that it achieves in *Reflections*.

3 Acting on instinct?

1   According to Marilyn Ann Moss, 'Actual shooting [of *A Place in the Sun*] began on October 4, 1949 on the Paramount lot and moved to Lake Tahoe, Nevada for location shooting in January 1950' (Moss, 2004, p. 163). That would make Taylor seventeen, not sixteen, when she first started working on the picture.

2   Taylor also states with regard to her own acting that: 'If I am portraying something emotional in a scene, I sweat real sweat and I shake real shakes' (1964, p. 162).

4 Compassion

1   In an interview with Peter Lawford in a documentary entitled *Elizabeth Taylor – An Intimate Portrait*, Richard Brooks claims that the suffering the

actress was undergoing as a result of the tragedy of Mike Todd's death induced her to learn how to draw on her own personal experiences in her acting:

Death and anguish were things that she read in a script and she tried to emulate from seeing other performances, from something that she could be told about. After all … she was a kid. Not much had happened in her life … to the extremes. And here was something that was happening to her at that time. And she was enough of a pro, and enough of an actress to know that this was something that you use, that you use honourably, and that you use to the best of its advantage. Because to be the best that you can all of the time, every time you come to bat … was part of her credo, at least as far as I know. And the two times I worked with her, that was what she believed and that's what she used. And she used everything in her life, finally, from that moment on, I think, and maybe even before. But she consciously used it from that time on. She knew that … someone may have to have fifteen rehearsals and that was fine with her. She, each one could work his or her way, whichever way they would, but she herself would use each and every incident of her life, of her experience, from that time on, it was a matter of just asking her to dig in to her own background. (1975)

Of her experience on *Cat* following Todd's death, Taylor, by contrast, writes: 'I couldn't tolerate what I was, and it gave me somebody else to become. When I was Maggie was the only time I could function' (1964, p. 86). In general, she repeatedly stresses her dislike of the Method approach whereby 'actors transplant themselves into a personal experience that they can identify with' (referring to it as 'a bit like cheating') and emphasises instead her conviction that 'if you are playing a part, you should not react the way you personally would react; you should react the way the character would react' (ibid., p. 164).

2   According to Garff B. Wilson, this 'emotionalistic' style of acting 'was developed almost exclusively by female performers' (1966, p. 110) and 'could be recognized by three dominant characteristics': (1) an approach whereby 'the actress … actually experienced the feelings and passions of

her role and surrendered herself to these emotions. She did not simulate but actively participated in the agonies of the mimicked character'. (2) The cultivation of 'a lush, overt display of the passions she was feeling' in a 'performance [that] was marked by sobs, tears, screams, shudders, heavings, writhings, pantings, growlings, tremblings, and all manner of physical manifestations'; and (3) 'neglect of technique' (ibid., pp. 110–11). He points out that the 'overlapping careers' of 'The five actresses who constitute this school' 'cover the period from 1845 … until 1929' and goes on to recount that:

This period embraces a long and significant segment of the history of the American stage, and these actresses [Anna Cora Mowatt, Laura Keene, Matilda Heron, Clara Morris and Mrs. Leslie Carter] are among the most significant and influential of their day. (Wilson, 1956)

Sara Sothern Taylor's main acting role (for which she won significant acclaim) was as the lame girl in Channing Pollock's stage melodrama *The Fool* and in his account of Elizabeth Taylor's performance in *National Velvet*, Alexander Walker suggests that 'the concentrated intensity of her emotion is, at times, eerily reminiscent of the photographs of her mother playing the little cripple in *The Fool*' (1990, p. 46).

Coda: Moving on

1 *Boom!* was adapted from Tennessee Williams's play *The Milk Train Doesn't Stop Here Anymore* (1963).
2 These tributes were widely quoted in the media. See, for example: www.parade.com/celebrity/hollywood-wire/2011/03/23/elizabeth-taylor-death-reaction.html.

BIBLIOGRAPHY

Affron, Charles, *Star Acting: Gish, Garbo, Davis* (New York: E. P. Dutton, 1977).

Affron, Charles, *Cinema and Sentiment* (Chicago, IL and London: University of Chicago Press, 1982).

Agee, James, *James Agee: Film Writing and Selected Journalism* (New York: Library of America, 2005).

Arnold, Maxine, 'Velvet Girl', *Photoplay* vol. 26 no. 6, May 1945, pp. 34–7, 90–1.

Asquith, Anthony, 'A Director Views Liz', *Los Angeles Times*, 1 September 1963, pp. 1, 7.

Astor, Mary, *Mary Astor: A Life on Film* (London: W. H. Allen, 1973).

Bagnold, Enid, *A Diary without Dates* (www.General-Books.net, 2009 [1918]).

Bagnold, Enid, *National Velvet* (London: Egmont Books Limited, 2000 [1935]).

Bagnold, Enid, *Enid Bagnold's Autobiography (from 1889)* (London: Century Publishing, 1985 [1969]).

Baker, Steve, *Picturing the Beast: Animals, Identity and Representation* (Urbana and Chicago: University of Illinois Press, 2001 [1993]).

Baron, Cynthia, 'Crafting Film Performances: Acting in the Hollywood Studio Era', in Alan Lovell and Peter Krämer (eds), *Screen Acting* (London and New York: Routledge, 1999), pp. 31–45.

Baron, Cynthia and Carnicke, Sharon Marie, *Reframing Screen Performance* (Ann Arbor: University of Michigan Press, 2008).

Baron, Cynthia and Warren, Beckett, 'The Actors Studio in the Early Cold War', in Cynthia Lucia, Roy Grundman and Art Simon (eds), *The Wiley-Blackwell History of American Film*, 1st edn (Malden, MA: Blackwell Publishing Ltd, 2011). Available online at: media.wiley.com/product_ancillary/48/14051798/ DOWNLOAD/Chapter%2047%20-%20The%20Actors%20Studio%20in%20the%20Early%20Cold%20War%20by%20Cynthia%20Baron%20and%20Beckett%20Warren.pdf.

Baron, Cynthia, Carson, Diane and Tomasulo, Frank P. (eds), *More than a Method: Trends and Traditions in Contemporary Film Performance* (Detroit, MI: Wayne State University Press, 2004).

Bosworth, Patricia, *Montgomery Clift: A Biography* (New York: Limelight Editions, 2007 [1978]).

Bozzacchi, Gianni, *Elizabeth Taylor: The Queen and I* (Madison: University of Wisconsin Press, 2002).

Bragg, Melvyn, *Rich: The Life of Richard Burton* (London: Hodder & Stoughton, 1988).

Burke, Liz, 'Elizabeth Taylor and *National Velvet*', Cinema and the Female Star – part 3, *Senses of Cinema* no. 60, 2002. Available online at: www.sensesofcinema.com/2002/23/symposium3/.

Burt, Jonathan, *Animals in Film* (London: Reaktion Books, 2002).

Calvo, Dana, 'A "Giant" Effort to Keep a Legacy Alive', *Los Angeles Times*, 9 June 2003.

Chapman, James and Cull, Nicholas, J., 'Facing the Stampede of Decolonization: *Elephant Walk* (1954)', in *Projecting Empire: Imperialism and Popular Cinema* (London: I. B. Tauris & Co Ltd, 2009), pp. 67–86.

Christopher, James, *Elizabeth Taylor: The Illustrated Biography* (London: Andre Deutsch, 1999).

Cronin, Paul (ed.), *George Stevens: Interviews* (Jackson: University Press of Mississippi, 2004).

Dauth, Brian (ed.), *Joseph L. Mankiewicz Interviews* (Jackson: University Press of Mississippi, 2008).

Dyer, Richard, 'First a Star: Elizabeth Taylor', in *Only Entertainment* (London and New York: Routledge, 1992), pp. 112–17.

Estrin, Allen, *The Hollywood Professionals Volume 6: Frank Capra, George Cukor, Clarence Brown* (South Brunswick, NJ and New York: A. S. Barnes and Company, 1980).

Friedan, Betty, *The Feminine Mystique* (London: Penguin Classics, 2010 [1963]).

Fudge, Erica, *Animal* (London: Reaktion Books, 2002).

Fudge, Erica, *Pets* (Stocksfield: Acumen Publishing, 2008).

Gardiner, Juliet, *The Animals' War: Animals in Wartime from the First World War to the Present Day* (London: Portrait in Association with the Imperial War Museum, 2006). Foreword by Jilly Cooper.

Gill, Brendan, 'The Current Cinema: The Impossible Takes Longer', *New Yorker*, 22 June 1963.

Halliwell, Martin, *American Culture in the 1950s* (Edinburgh: Edinburgh University Press, 2007).

Harris, Eleanor, 'The Elizabeth Taylor Story', *Look Magazine*, Part 1 of 3, 26 June 1956, pp. 119–23.

Harrison, Rex, *Rex: An Autobiography* (London: Book Club Associates, 1975).

Head, Edith and Calistro, Paddy, *Edith Head's Hollywood* (Santa Monica, CA: Angel City Press, 2008).

Heymann, C. David, *Liz: An Intimate Biography of Elizabeth Taylor* (New York: Carol Publishing Group, 1995).

Hirsch, Foster, *Elizabeth Taylor* (New York City: Galahad Books, 1973).

Hirsch, Foster, *Acting Hollywood Style* (New York: Harry N. Abrams, Inc., Publishers, 1991).

Hopper, Hedda, 'Debbie and Eddie Part in Spat on Liz Taylor', *Los Angeles Times*, 10 September 1958.

Hopper, Hedda, 'Liz Taylor's Own Story of Eddie's Marital Rift', *Los Angeles Times*, 11 September 1958.

Howe, Herb, 'Little Queen Bess', *Photoplay* vol. 28 no. 1, December 1945, pp. 1–2, 99–101.

Hozic, Aida A., 'Hollywood Goes on Sale: or, What Do the Violet Eyes of Elizabeth Taylor Have to Do with the "Cinema of Attractions"?', in David Desser and Gareth Jowett (eds), *Hollywood Goes Shopping* (Minneapolis and London: University of Minnesota Press, 2000), pp. 205–21.

Huston, John, *An Open Book* (Cambridge, MA: Da Capo Press, 1994 [1980]).

Kashner, Sam and Schoenberger, Nancy, *Furious Love: Elizabeth Taylor, Richard Burton, and the Marriage of the Century* (New York: HarperCollins Publishers, 2010).

Kelley, Kitty, *Elizabeth Taylor: The Last Star* (New York: Simon and Schuster, 1981).

Klevan, Andrew, *Film Performance: From Achievement to Appreciation* (London: Wallflower Press, 2005).

Knight, Arthur, 'A Liz Taylor Festival', *Saturday Review*, 28 October 1967.

Lambert, Gavin, *The Ivan Moffat File: Life among the Beautiful and Damned in London, Paris, New York and Hollywood* (New York: Pantheon Books, 2004).

Lawrence, Amy, *The Passion of Montgomery Clift* (Berkeley, Los Angeles and London: University of California Press, 2010).

Leigh, Janet, *There Really Was a Hollywood: An Autobiography* (Garden City, NY: Doubleday & Company, Inc., 1984).

Long, Robert Emmet (ed.), *John Huston Interviews* (Jackson: University Press of Mississippi, 2002).

Lowe, Herb, 'Liz Takes French Leave', *Photoplay* vol. 45 no. 6, June 1954, pp. 44–5, 113–15.

Lower, Cheryl Bray and Palmer, R. Barton, *Joseph L. Mankiewicz: Critical Essays with an Annotated Bibliography and a Filmography* (Jefferson, NC, and London: McFarland & Company, Inc., Publishers, 2001).

Lury, Karen, *The Child in Film: Tears, Fears and Fairy Tales* (London: I. B. Tauris, 2010).

McCann, Graham, *Rebel Males: Clift, Brando and Dean* (London: Hamish Hamilton, 1991).

Maddox, Brenda, *Who's Afraid of Elizabeth Taylor?* (London: Granada Publishing Limited, 1979 [1977]).

Mann, William, J., *How to Be a Movie Star: Elizabeth Taylor in Hollywood* (London: Faber and Faber Limited, 2009).

Mason, Bruce, Letter to John Huston, *John Huston Special Collection*, Margaret Herrick Library, 19 February 1969.

Miller, D. A., 'Visual Pleasure in 1959', *October* no. 81, Summer 1997, pp. 35–58.

Moss, Marilyn Ann, *Giant: George Stevens, a Life on Film* (Madison: University of Wisconsin Press, 2004).

Munn, Michael, *Richard Burton: Prince of Players* (London: J. R. Books, 2009).

O'Connor, Jane, *The Cultural Significance of the Child Star* (New York and London: Routledge, 2008).

Ohi, Kevin, 'Devouring Creation: Cannibalism, Sodomy, and the Scene of Analysis in *Suddenly, Last Summer*', *Cinema Journal* vol. 38 no. 3, Spring 1999, pp. 27–49.

Paglia, Camille, *Sex, Art and American Culture* (New York: Vintage Books, 1992).

Paller, Michael, 'The Day on Which a Woman Dies: *The Milk Train Doesn't Stop Here Anymore* and No Theatre', in Philip C. Kolin (ed.), *The Undiscovered Country: The Later Plays of Tennessee Williams* (New York: Peter Lang Publishing, 2002), pp. 25–39.

Polito, Robert (ed.), *Farber on Film: The Complete Film Writings of Manny Farber* (New York: Library of America: 2009).

Pollock, Channing, *The Fool: A Play in Four Acts* (London and New York: Samuel French, 1922).

Reynolds, Debbie and Columbia, David Patrick, *Debbie: My Life* (London: Sidgwick & Jackson, 1989).

Rooney, Mickey, *Life Is Too Short* (New York: Villard Books, 1991).

Russo, Vito, *The Celluloid Closet: Homosexuality in the Movies*, revised edn (New York: Harper & Row Publishers, 1987).

Scheiner, Georganne, *Signifying Female Adolescence: Film Representations and Fans, 1920–1950* (Westport, CT and London: Praeger, 2000).

Schickel, Richard, 'A Movie Whose Ambitions Were as Big as All Outdoors', *New York Times*, 15 May 2003.

Schoenberger, Nancy, interview with James Adams, '"A Game Girl": Liz Taylor Biographer Recalls Star's Tumultuous Life', *Globe and Mail*, 25 March 2011. Available online at: <m.theglobeandmail.com/news/arts/books/

a-game-girl-liz-taylor-biographer-recalls-stars-tumultuous-life/
article1956645/?service=mobile.

Service, Faith [Gladys Hall], 'Vaguely Wonderful', *Photoplay* vol. 47 no. 6,
February 1955, pp. 54–5, 76–7.

Smith, Susan, '"Get off Your Asses for These Old Broads!": Elizabeth Taylor,
Ageing and the Television Comeback Movie', *Celebrity Studies* vol. 3 no. 1,
2012.

Snow, Nancy E., 'Compassion', *American Philosophical Quarterly* vol. 28 no. 3,
July 1991, pp. 195–205.

Spoto, Donald, *Elizabeth Taylor* (London: Little, Brown and Company, 1995).

Steinem, Gloria, 'Suggestions for the Promotion of "Reflections in a Golden
Eye" Plus Some Totally Unsolicited Comments', John Huston Special
Collection (undated), Margaret Herrick Library, Academy of Motion
Picture Arts and Sciences, pp. 1–6.

Studlar, Gaylyn, 'Elizabeth Taylor and Virginal English Girlhood', in Tamar
Jeffers McDonald (ed.), *Virgin Territory: Representing Sexual Inexperience in
Film* (Detroit, MI: Wayne State University Press, 2010), pp. 15–33.

Taraborrelli, J. Randy, *Elizabeth* (London: Pan Books, 2006).

Taylor, Elizabeth, 'Nibbles and Me', *Photoplay* vol. 29 no. 3, August 1946,
pp. 1–5.

Taylor, Elizabeth, *Nibbles and Me* (New York: Simon and Schuster, 2002
[Duell, Sloan and Pearce, Inc., 1946]).

Taylor, Elizabeth, *Elizabeth Taylor: An Informal Memoir by Elizabeth Taylor*
(New York: Harper & Row, Publishers, 1964).

Taylor, Elizabeth, *Elizabeth Takes Off* (London: Macmillan, 1988).

Taylor, Elizabeth, *Elizabeth Taylor: My Love Affair with Jewelry* (London:
Thames & Hudson, 2002).

Temple Black, Shirley, *Child Star: An Autobiography* (London: Headline Book
Publishing, 1989).

Thiltges, Alexander, *Elizabeth Taylor: A Life in Pictures* (London: Pavilion
Books, 2008).

Ursini, James, *Elizabeth Taylor: The Last True Hollywood Diva* (Los Angeles,
CA: Taschen, 2008).

Walker, Alexander, *Elizabeth: The Life of Elizabeth Taylor* (New York: Grove Press, 1990).

Waterbury, Ruth with Arceri, Gene, *Elizabeth Taylor: Her Life, Her Loves, Her Future* (New York: Bantam Books, 1982 [1964]).

Webster, Noah, *A Dictionary of the English Language, Vol. I* [New York: Black and Young, 1828]. Cited in *Webster's Online Dictionary*. Available online at: www.websters-online-dictionary.org/definitions/instinctive.

Williams, Dick, 'Liz Is a Whiz as a Grandmother', *Mirror News*, 26 September 1955.

Williams, Tennessee, *Cat on a Hot Tin Roof* (London: Penguin Books, 2009 [1956]).

Williams, Tennessee, *Suddenly, Last Summer and Other Plays* (London: Penguin Books, 2009 [1958]).

Williams, Tennessee, *Memoirs* (London: Penguin Books, 2007 [1972]).

Wilson, Garff, B. 'Emotionalism in Acting', *Quarterly Journal of Speech* vol. 42 no. 1, 1956. Available online at: www.tandfonline.com/doi/abs/10.1080/00335635609382123?journalCode=rqjs20.

Wilson, Garff B. *A History of American Acting* (Bloomington and London: Indiana University Press, 1966).

Wilson, Garff B., *Three Hundred Years of American Drama and Theatre: From Ye Bare and Ye Cubb to Chorus Line* (Englewood Cliffs, NJ: Prentice-Hall, Inc., 1973).

Winston, Robert, *Human Instinct: How Our Primeval Impulses Shape Our Modern Lives* (London: Bantam Press, 2002).

Anonymous

Article by female fan entitled 'Lovely Lady from London' (anon), Bennett Tarleton collection of fan club newsletters, 1: 9 (Summer 1958b), Margaret Herrick Library, Academy of Motion Picture Arts and Sciences.

'Girl Jockey W ...: National Velvet' [partial title only], *L.A. Tidings*, 2 February 1945.

Letter from female fan to Hedda Hopper (anon), Elizabeth Taylor files, Hedda
Hopper papers (10 September 1958a), Margaret Herrick Library,
Academy of Motion Picture Arts and Sciences.

'National Velvet', *Variety*, daily issue, 6 December 1944a.

Program Notes for *National Velvet*, Metro-Goldwyn-Mayer (1944c).

'Tremendous Drama of Color, Spectacle; Berman Prod. Great', *Hollywood
Reporter*, 6 December 1944b.

Unsourced, untitled review of *Reflections in a Golden Eye*, 4 December 1967,
p. 33.

Other

Berman, Pandro, *Pandro S. Berman: A Louis B. Mayer Foundation-American
Film Institute Oral History*, conducted and prepared by Mike Steen
(Hollywood, CA: American Film Institute, 1972).

Burns Sidney, Lillian, *Oral History Collection on the Performing Arts/Southern
Methodist University*, interview conducted by Ronald L. Davis (Dallas, TX:
Southern Methodist University [1986] 1988).

Callow, Ridgeway, *Oral History with Ridgeway Callow*/interviewed by Rudy
Behlmer, American Film Institute Film History Program (Beverly Hills,
CA: Center for Advanced Film Studies, American Film Institute, 1976).

Television and documentary programmes

What's My Line?, CBS television series, guest appearance by Elizabeth Taylor,
14 November 1954. Available online at: www.youtube.com/results?
search_query=what%27s+my+line+elizabeth+taylor&aq=f.

Edward R. Murrow *Person to Person* television show, season 4, episode 30,
interview with Elizabeth Taylor and Mike Todd (CBS News, originally
aired 5 April 1957). Available on the DVD collection *Edward R. Murrow:
The Best of Person to Person* (CBS/Koch Entertainment LP, 2006).

Elizabeth Taylor – An Intimate Portrait (Jack Haley, Jr. Productions, Inc., 1975).

Taylor, Elizabeth, *21st American Film Institute Lifetime Achievement Award* (1993). First aired on ABC network. For the tribute address, see: www.afi.com/laa/laa93.aspx. Extract showing Taylor's receipt of the award available online at: www.youtube.com/watch?v=5GSOUusJHOM.

Elizabeth Taylor: England's Other Elizabeth (Kultur, 2001: D2170). A PBS programme originally aired on 4 April 2001. Further details available online at: www.pbs.org/wnet/gperf/shows/elizabethtaylor.html.

George Stevens and His Place in the Sun (2001), extra on DVD of *A Place in the Sun* (Stevens, 1951) (Paramount Home Entertainment, 2002).

The Elizabeth Taylor Story (Produced by Prometheus Entertainment and Foxstar Productions in association with Fox Television Studios and A&E Network, 2003). Aired on 24 March 2011 on the Biography Channel under the title 'BIO Remembers: Elizabeth Taylor'.

Paul Newman, tribute to Elizabeth Taylor (Classic Turner Movies channel, 2007). Available online at: www.youtube.com/watch?v= NyHa4NSmTkk&feature=related.

FILMOGRAPHY

THERE'S ONE BORN EVERY MINUTE (Harold Young, US, 1942),
Gloria Twine

LASSIE COME HOME (Fred M. Wilcox, US, 1943), Priscilla

JANE EYRE (Robert Stevenson, US, 1944), [uncredited] Helen Burns

THE WHITE CLIFFS OF DOVER (Clarence Brown, US, 1944),
[uncredited] Betsy Kenney, age 10

NATIONAL VELVET (Clarence Brown, US, 1944), Velvet Brown

COURAGE OF LASSIE (Fred M. Wilcox, US, 1946), Kathie Eleanor
Merrick

LIFE WITH FATHER (Michael Curtiz, US, 1947), Mary Skinner

CYNTHIA (Robert Z. Leonard, US, 1947), Cynthia Bishop

A DATE WITH JUDY (Richard Thorpe, US, 1948), Carol Pringle

JULIA MISBEHAVES (Jack Conway, US, 1948), Susan Packett

LITTLE WOMEN (Mervyn LeRoy, US, 1949), Amy

CONSPIRATOR (Victor Saville, UK, 1950), Melinda Greyton

FATHER OF THE BRIDE (Vincente Minnelli, US, 1950), Kay Banks

THE BIG HANGOVER (Norman Krasna, US, 1950), Mary Belney

FATHER'S LITTLE DIVIDEND (Vincente Minnelli, US, 1951), Kay

A PLACE IN THE SUN (George Stevens, US, 1951), Angela Vickers

QUO VADIS (Mervyn LeRoy, US, 1951) [uncredited appearance]

LOVE IS BETTER THAN EVER (Stanley Donen, US, 1952), Anastacia
Macaboy

IVANHOE (Richard Thorpe, US, 1952), Rebecca

THE GIRL WHO HAD EVERYTHING (Richard Thorpe, US, 1953), Jean Latimer

RHAPSODY (Charles Vidor, US, 1954), Louise Durant

ELEPHANT WALK (William Dieterle, US, 1954), Ruth Wiley

BEAU BRUMMELL (Curtis Bernhardt, UK, 1954), Lady Patricia

THE LAST TIME I SAW PARIS (Richard Brooks, US, 1954), Helen Ellswirth

GIANT (George Stevens, US, 1956), Leslie Lynnton Benedict

RAINTREE COUNTY (Edward Dmytryk, US, 1957), Susanna Drake Shawnessy

CAT ON A HOT TIN ROOF (Richard Brooks, US, 1958), Maggie Pollitt

SUDDENLY, LAST SUMMER (Joseph L. Mankiewicz, UK/US, 1959), Catherine Holly

SCENT OF MYSTERY (Jack Cardiff, US, 1960) [uncredited], the real Sally

BUTTERFIELD 8 (Daniel Mann, US, 1960), Gloria Wandrous

CLEOPATRA (Joseph L. Mankiewicz, UK/US, 1963), Cleopatra

THE V.I.P.S (Anthony Asquith, US/UK, 1963), Frances Andros

THE SANDPIPER (Vincente Minnelli, US, 1965), Laura Reynolds

WHO'S AFRAID OF VIRGINIA WOOLF? (Mike Nichols, US, 1966), Martha

THE TAMING OF THE SHREW (Franco Zeffirelli, Italy/US, 1967), Katharina

REFLECTIONS IN A GOLDEN EYE (John Huston, UK/US, 1967), Leonora Penderton

DOCTOR FAUSTUS (Richard Burton, Nevill Coghill, UK/Italy, 1967), Helen

THE COMEDIANS (Peter Glenville, US/Bermuda/France, 1967), Martha Pineda

BOOM! (Joseph Losey, UK/US, 1968), Flora 'Sissy' Goforth

SECRET CEREMONY (Joseph Losey, UK/US, 1968), Leonora

ANNE OF THE THOUSAND DAYS (Charles Jarrott, UK/US, 1969) [uncredited], [courtesan]

THE ONLY GAME IN TOWN (George Stevens, US, 1970), Fran Walker
UNDER MILK WOOD (Andrew Sinclair, UK, 1971), Rosie Probert
X, Y AND ZEE (Brian G. Hutton, UK, 1972), Zee Blakeley
HAMMERSMITH IS OUT (Peter Ustinov, US, 1972), Jimmie Jean Jackson
DIVORCE HIS/DIVORCE HERS (Waris Hussein, UK, 1973, TV), Jane
    Reynolds
NIGHT WATCH (Brian G. Hutton, US, 1973), Ellen Wheeler
ASH WEDNESDAY (Larry Peerce, US, 1973), Barbara Sawyer
IDENTIKIT aka THE DRIVER'S SEAT (Giuseppe Patroni Griffi, Italy,
    1974), Lise
THE BLUE BIRD (George Cukor, US/USSR, 1976), mother/Maternal
    Love/witch/Light
VICTORY AT ENTEBBE (Marvin Chomsky, US, 1976, TV), Edra
    Vilnofsky
A LITTLE NIGHT MUSIC (Harold Prince, 1978), Desiree Armfeldt
RETURN ENGAGEMENT (Joseph Hardy, US, 1978, TV), Dr Emily
    Loomis
WINTER KILLS (William Richert, US, 1979), [uncredited] Lola Comante
THE MIRROR CRACK'D (Guy Hamilton, UK, 1980), Marina Gregg
GENOCIDE (Arnold Schwartzman, US, 1982), [narrator]
BETWEEN FRIENDS (Lou Antonio, US, 1983, TV), Deborah Shapiro
MALICE IN WONDERLAND (Gus Trikonis, US, 1985, TV), Louella
    Parsons
NORTH AND SOUTH (Richard T. Heffron, 1985, TV), Madam Conti
THERE MUST BE A PONY (Joseph Sargent, US, 1986, TV), Marguerite
    Sydney
POKER ALICE (Arthur A. Seidelman, US, 1987, TV), Alice Moffit
IL GIOVANE TOSCANINI (Franco Zeffirelli, Italy/France/US, 1988),
    Nadina Bulichoff
SWEET BIRD OF YOUTH (Nicolas Roeg, US, 1989, TV), Alexandra Del
    Lago
THE FLINTSTONES (Brian Levant, US, 1994), Pearl Slaghoople
THESE OLD BROADS (Matthew Diamond, 2001, US, TV), Beryl Mason

Television series

GENERAL HOSPITAL (1981), Helena Cassadine

ALL MY CHILDREN (1983, 1984), Boardmember at the Chateau, Maid at the Goal Post Restaurant

HOTEL (1984), Katherine Cole

CAPTAIN PLANET AND THE PLANETEERS (1992), Mrs Andrews

THE SIMPSONS (1992, 1993), Maggie Simpson [voice], Herself [voice]

GOD, THE DEVIL AND BOB (2003), Sarah

INDEX

Note: Page numbers in **bold** indicate detailed analysis; those in *italic* denote illustrations. *n* = endnote.

List of illustrations

While considerable effort has been made to correctly identify the copyright holders, this has not been possible in all cases. We apologise for any apparent negligence and any omissions or corrections brought to our attention will be remedied in any future editions.